Total Design
Sourcebook

Display

A RotoVision Book
Published and distributed by RotoVision SA
Route Suisse 9
CH-1295 Mies
Switzerland

RotoVision SA
Sales and Editorial Office
Sheridan House, 114 Western Road
Hove BN3 1DD, UK
Tel: +44 (0)1273 72 72 68
Fax: +44 (0)1273 72 72 69
www.rotovision.com

10 9 8 7 6 5 4 3 2 1
ISBN: 978-2-88893-010-5

Art Director for RotoVision Tony Seddon
Design by Form (www.form.uk.com)

Reprographics in Singapore by ProVision Pte.
Tel: +65 6334 7720
Fax: +65 6334 7721

Printed in Singapore by Star Standard Industries (Pte.) Ltd

Total Design
Sourcebook

Display

**2-D and 3-D Design for Exhibitions,
Galleries, Museums, and Trade Shows**
John Stones

RotoVision

Contents

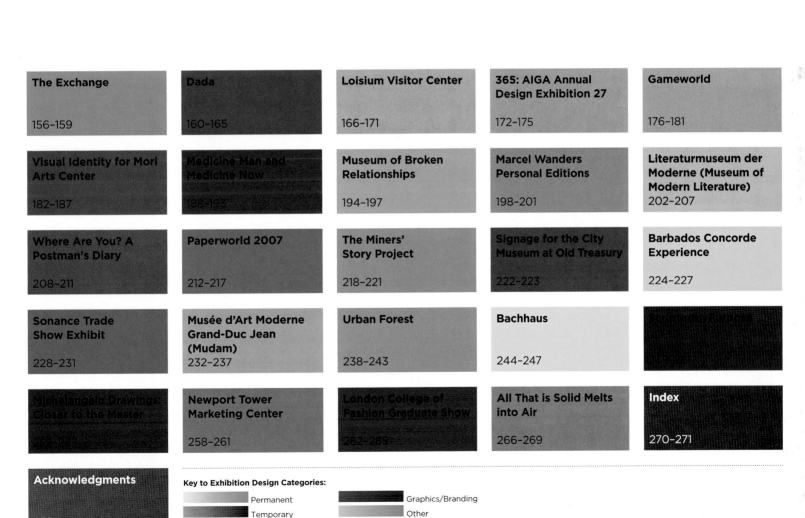

Key to Exhibition Design Categories:

Permanent

Temporary

Trade

Graphics/Branding

Other

Introduction

Exhibitions are an increasingly important part of our lives. Part of a mass spectacle, they compete with movies, advertising, shopping, sports, and television for attention. And as exhibitions, whether small temporary shows, trade shows, or grand museums, jostle for room, presentation has become almost as important as the objects presented themselves. Visitors want and expect a memorable and engaging experience, elevating the importance of the exhibition design. No longer can a display depend purely on the exhibited object.

Architecture, as the most privileged area of design, has been in the vanguard. But the full range of design disciplines are being called upon to create these experiences. Websites and interactive stations, signage, graphics, illustration, catalogs, merchandise, logotypes, and marketing materials, all can be as much part of the experience as the actual exhibition design and architecture. Increasingly, these distinctions are blurred as the approach becomes more holistic, and, sometimes, the most innovative solutions come from designers (or artists) who normally operate in different fields.

Regardless of the approach, designing exhibitions can be uniquely rewarding—unlike some design projects, there is an audience that comes with open and receptive eyes. As Kai-Uwe Bergmann of Danish architects BIG, which staged an innovative exhibition of its work in New York (see pages 54–57) points out, "When as an architect you build something, only a few people will experience it physically. For most it will just be a picture in a book or magazine. With an exhibition, you get somewhere in between."

No discussion of contemporary exhibition design can take place without mention of the phenomenal success of the Frank Gehry-designed Guggenheim Museum in Bilbao. But its undeniable impact has earlier precedents. Think of the Great Exhibition held in the Crystal Palace in London in 1851 (which was then replicated in New York), or the Entartete Kunst (Degenerate Art) show staged in Nazi Germany. Ironically, this contemptuous display of "degenerate" art has much more in common with the display designs of our own times. The show also managed to attract millions of visitors, considerably more than the concurrent exhibition of ideal Nazi art in the temple-like display of Haus der Deutschen Kunst in Munich.

But perhaps the best examples of display are the Gothic cathedrals of France. The full spectrum of creative skills was brought into play by medieval artisans, creating all kinds of exhibition objects,

Left: Hairywood, 6a architects and Eley Kishimoto for The Architecture Foundation, London. Photo by David Grandorge.

from stained glass narratives to elaborate reliquaries containing holy remains, all housed in architecture that still manages to inspire awe some 700 years on.

As with the cathedrals, an interdisciplinary approach is increasingly characteristic of display today, with borrowings from the neighboring disciplines of theater, film, and art. But there are also the many side chapels, those little shows whose lack of size can often permit greater freedom and creative flexibility.

Of course, the word display can have negative connotations, suggesting a peacock-like ostentation. For many, the mark of a good exhibition design is that a visitor doesn't notice it in his or her appreciation of the objects on display. But, more recently, the exhibition designer's contribution has moved further center stage, as design increases in stature and public recognition. A good many visitors to, say, the Bilbao Guggenheim, San Francisco Museum of Modern Art, or Centre Pompidou in Paris will be aware of the architect responsible for the eye-catching structures. Indeed, in some cases, this will even be the main reason for visiting the museum. Steven Holl's Bloch Building extension to the Nelson-Atkins Museum of Art (see pages 120–125) will have got many non-US citizens getting maps out wondering how they can get to

Kansas City. More and more, this same attention will be given to the role of designers other than architects.

Good exhibition design traditionally has conformed to one of two approaches. Remaining true to the primary object of display, the self-effacing exhibition design is either narrative in structure, informing the visitor of background information and contextualizing the objects in a story, or emotive, remaining true to the objects by presenting an environment that is immersive, recreating a relevant and affecting context.

Alongside these approaches, new, more self-referential exhibition designs are being implemented. These can clamor for attention as persuasively as the display objects themselves, either by adopting interactive or theatrical approaches.

And more radical and controversial still, is the parallel approach, where two equal experiences are on offer, one being the exhibition, and the other the designed environment in which this takes place. Perhaps Jean Nouvel's Musée du quai Branly (see pages 48–53) in Paris falls into this category, with its controversial renunciation of contemporary norms of museology in the creation of an aesthetically fascinating environment. The beauty and aesthetic pleasure of the exhibition

Top, left: Medicine Man and Medicine Now, Gitta Gschwendtner and Kerr Noble for Wellcome Trust, London. Photo by Sorted.

Top, right: Bloch Building, Nelson-Atkins Museum of Art by Steven Holl Architects, Kansas City. Photo by Andy Ryan.

space becomes simply a bonus, a side dish that can either complement or overpower the main dish, but gorgeous in its own right.

Whether this is a friction between architecture and exhibition design, an abdication of exhibition design, or perhaps the emergence of a new kind of space, is the subject of debate. It is naturally the big museums and galleries, supported with extensive marketing, that are in the spotlight here, but it is a trend you can see across the board, spilling into the smallest temporary exhibition too.

But traditional narrative exhibition design is not immune to commercial pressures. Either these narrative displays can be executed dutifully by conscientious exhibition designers, or they can be theme parks, less profound—even superficial—displays, harking back to another tradition, that of the circus or waxwork show. "What makes an exhibition different is the element of authenticity. It is theater versus film. Or the theme park versus the museum," suggests Stephen Greenberg, director of London-based Metaphor, responsible for the design of many important exhibitions (such as Michelangelo Drawings: Closer to the Master, see pages 252–257) and currently masterplanning the Grand Egyptian Museum due to open in Giza next to

the pyramids in 2010. Of course, the largest exhibitions, whether permanent or temporary, are in direct competition with other big budget entertainments. "It's not Hollywood—but some of the production values are the same," says Greenberg. Like other larger exhibition design companies, his firm regularly carries out consumer clinics, in the same way as a large movie studio or car manufacturer might, to test how well a particular design will or has worked.

Interactivity has been a buzz word in the exhibitions world for some time. But the actual interactive experience has rarely met the claims or hopes of the client or designers. The dot com era of blue-lit, computerized interactivity has quickly become as dated as stuffed birds in glass cases, and designers have teased out new, less structured ways of creating more genuinely interactive experiences. Perhaps the most radical is the Museum of Broken Relationships (see pages 194–197), a traveling and online show created by two Croatian artists, in which visitors supply the objects and captions. Projects such as the Miners' Story Project, a trailer that toured Arizona and New Mexico collecting and sharing local stories (see pages 218–221), and the Medicine Now exhibition at the Wellcome Collection in London (see pages 188–193), which has interactives that mix lo-tech pads and

"As well as the interaction between display and visitors, another form of interaction is often crucial—that between the different designers."

pencils with creative uses of computer technology, point the way to some of the possibilities that will surely be even more fully exploited as technological advances such as RFID (radio frequency identification) tags are more seamlessly integrated into designs.

As well as the interaction between display and visitors, another form of interaction is often crucial—that between the different designers and experts typically involved in the creation of an exhibition. While publicly parties will usually claim the collaboration was fruitful and problem free, the truth can be one of egos being crushed and constant rancor. When designers choose to work together, however, sometimes genuine collaborations worthy of the name do take place, such as in the intriguing Hairywood installation in London (see pages 150–155). Tellingly, the designers (architects 6a and fashion designers Eley Kishimoto) had successfully collaborated before.

Collaboration is not an option but a necessity on a larger project, where typically there will be in-house curatorial and exhibition staff working with freelance curators and exhibition designers, who in turn will be working with a series of collaborators, from graphic designers and model makers to creators of digital interactions or animations, or from lighting consultants to fabrication specialists, and so on. This is not to mention the marketing teams, interpretation specialists, accessibility consultants, and copyright lawyers who might typically also be brought in, particularly on high profile projects. The difficulty of retaining a creative edge in the face of these committees means that the big names do not always have it all their own way.

The following projects exemplify the many different forms, disciplines, and approaches that are currently at work in exhibition design, from some of the most innovative and creative practitioners today. From the smallest exhibition executed on a shoestring, to the multimillion projects supported by governments, each is intended to inspire, inform, or entertain in some way. Enjoy the show.

Right: CPH Experiments, Bjarke Ingels Group (BIG) for Storefront for Art and Architecture, New York. Photo by BIG.

The High Style of Dorothy Draper

"Keeping one of Draper's famous quips in mind— 'If it looks right it is right'— we decided to create an environment that we hoped would surprise and delight visitors much as Draper's work had, by further exaggerating scale."

Urshula Barbour, Pure+Applied

Far left: Entrance to the exhibition, with oversized sampling from Draper's own designs on the wall and a hanging panel with script redrawn from the logo of Dorothy Draper & Co. The table and chairs are reproduction Draper items.

Left: Head-on view of the Hampshire House doors. Both photos by Harry Zernike.

"All the minor furniture of the show was related to the designs of Dorothy Draper in spirit rather than being out and out pastiche."

"Startle visitors" was the essence of the brief given to Pure+Applied by Donald Albrecht, the curator of an exhibition dedicated to the oversize personality of Dorothy Draper, the interior design queen of the 1940s and 1950s.

"We chose not to simply recreate a Draper room or rooms. Rather, keeping one of Draper's famous quips in mind—'If it looks right it is right'—we decided to create an environment that we hoped would surprise and delight visitors much as Draper's work had, by further exaggerating scale," says Urshula Barbour.

Using cues from Draper's own projects, a series of "moments" were planned, all using the Draper palette of colors. As visitors entered the rotunda, they were greeted by an intense cactus flower pink ceiling, 4 foot (1.2 meter) wide roses (based on Draper's Manor Rose pattern), and white silhouettes of her plasterwork

Top, right: View down the first hallway, showing the walls in the broad stripes of The Greenbrier. Photo by Museum of the City of New York.

Above, right: Forced perspective was used in the installation of four sets of recreated Hampshire House doors. Photo by Harry Zernike.

The High Style of Dorothy Draper

shapes on a black ground. Reproductions of her furniture were present for people to experience at first hand. Barbour and partner Paul Carlos redrew the hand-drawn script used for the logo of Dorothy Draper & Co and used it for the hanging title panel.

The visitor would then look down the hallway, decked out in the broad stripes Draper used for The Greenbrier Hotel, to see the (original) fuchsia Dorotheum sofa and white birdcage chandelier at the other end. At the end of the hallway lay another surprise. Four sets of Hampshire House doors were built and installed atop a black-and-white checkerboard floor, both designed in a forced perspective. Again, all the minor furniture of the show was related to the designs of Dorothy Draper in spirit rather than being out and out pastiche. For instance, in a nod to Draper's use of chinoiserie, all the photographs in the show are presented in thin gold frames with onyx black mats. The same thinking lay behind the choice of Mrs. Eaves as the typeface for the exhibition. "Its numerous ligatures suggested to us the shapes of Draper's elaborate plasterwork creations," says Barbour.

Lead designers: Urshula Barbour and Paul Carlos
Lighting: Anita Jorgensen

Left: The fuchsia Dorotheum sofa
and white birdcage chandelier,
originally designed for the
Metropolitan Museum of Art, were
framed at the end of the hallway
against a field of deep Gondola
Ride green. Photo by Harry Zernike.

Above: The oversize Manor Rose pattern was painted for the show by Millree Hughes and also appeared on all the arches.

Right: Overview showing the interconnections between different parts of the show. Both photos by Museum of the City of New York.

The High Style of Dorothy Draper

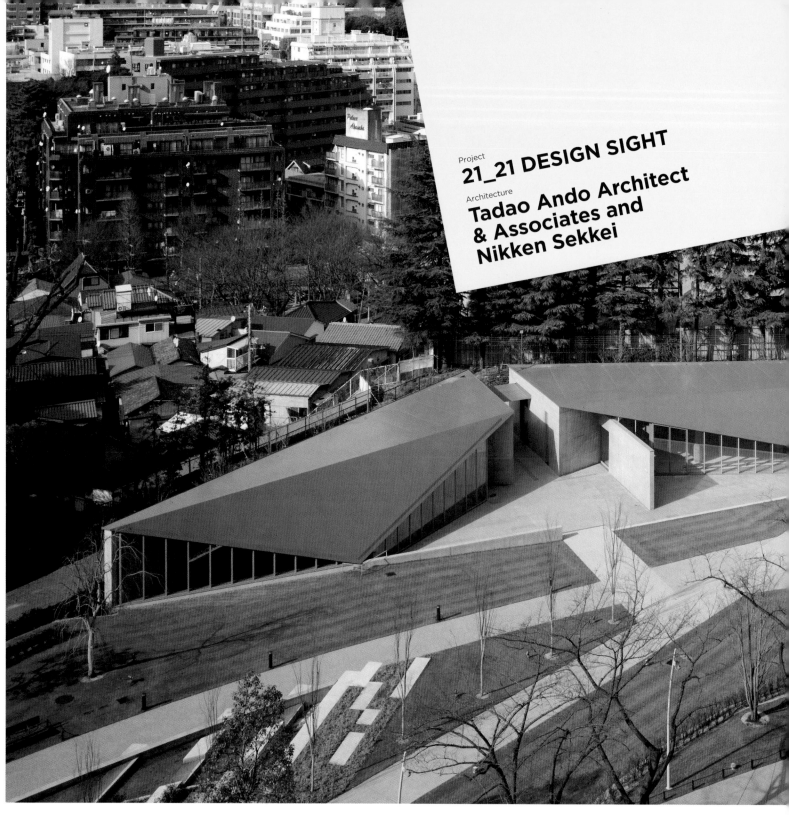

Project
21_21 DESIGN SIGHT

Architecture
Tadao Ando Architect & Associates and Nikken Sekkei

Client
The Issey Miyake Foundation

Location
Tokyo

"The roof, welded together to seem like a single piece, is taken as a reference to Miyake's 'one piece of cloth' approach to design, and allows the building to relate with delicacy to its immediate environment."

Left: Aerial view of the 21_21 DESIGN SIGHT complex in landscaped gardens, part of the Tokyo Midtown development in Roppongi.

Tokyo's first design museum is the brainchild of fashion designer Issey Miyake. Rather than a static repository for design objects, it is intended as a showcase for the design process. Or in its own words, it is "a research center for design, a place for thinking about design, and a place where things are actually made." Consequently, the talents of some of Japan's greatest designers were harnessed for the project.

Apart from the architecture of Tadao Ando, and the creative direction of product designer Naoto Fukasawa, there is also the input of graphic designer Taku Satoh, responsible for 21_21 DESIGN SIGHT's identity and communications, as well as exhibition design. Both Fukasawa and Satoh sit on the board of 21_21 DESIGN SIGHT alongside Miyake.

Satoh's distinctive baby blue logo is made of pressed metal and is reminiscent of number plates. As well as existing as a "product" in its own right, the visual identity has the virtue of standing out against the austere concrete of Ando's architecture and being versatile for a number of applications. For instance, 21_21 DESIGN SIGHT has "outdoor shops" which are essentially Nissan Cube cars. After being converted by the Nissan Design Center, these are parked outside in the center's grounds and decked out in humorous

Above, left: The center's corporate identity, taking the form of a number plate, allows it to be placed on the actual building or on graphic communications with equal ease.

Top, right: A dramatic staircase descends below ground into a space defined by polished concrete and 36 foot (11 meter) glass panels.

Above, right: The sloping roofs allow for a discreet presence.

第2回企画展
佐藤 卓 ディレクション
EXHIBITION 2 DIRECTED BY TAKU SATOH
コンセプト・スーパーバイザー：竹村真一
CONCEPT SUPERVISOR : SHINICHI TAKEMURA

water
［水・mizu］

What can design show us about our society, and the natural world that surrounds us? This "water" exhibition has been organized according five themes, developed from research and a vibrant discourse among a multi-disciplinary development team. Additionally, publications, web sites, public discourses and workshops will attempt to extend this multi-sensory experiment beyond the confines of the exhibition venue to help understand how design can illuminate the role of water in our lives.

A Water Memories
An attempt to extract the "core aquatic experiences" from our individual awareness, and at the same time, to renew an intrinsic meme for the Japanese, whose culture has always been informed by water.

B Water Magic
Water is a constitutive element of our world, a magical substance that enables life. Context design helps us discover new aspects both of water that is unseen, and of the water that we thought we knew.

C A History of Water
Where does this, or that water come from? What memories does it bear? An attempt at accurately visualizing the "water hood" that surrounds us.

D The Water Planet
The 21st century had been called "the water century". Here we attempt to create a visceral literacy through real-time data about the living planet.

E The Water City
By augmenting our maps to include the city as water experiences it, we are taken outside of the exhibition hall to rediscover how Tokyo itself already presents a rich water exhibition.

21_21

Works with the star mark (★) are collaborative works by the "water" exhibition creative team. Names listed on this page denote the primary instigating members for a given work within the team.

(1) **Rising water**
Tamotsu Fujii

(2) **kotobana**

(3) **water circle**
Arakawakensuke, Nozomu Miura

(4) **Tangible water planet**
Shinichi Takemura

(5) **SKY WATER HARVESTERS**
Makoto Murase (Dr. Rainwater)

(6) **water trace : tap sensware**
Shinichi Takemura

(7) **HOH**
Haruki Kaio, Hiroaki Ide

(8) **Virtual Water Server** ★ (Mobile version → 26)
Shinichi Takemura, Taku Satoh

UTSU-WA Works (1) ~ (26)
Taku Satoh

(9) **Twirling Planet** ★

(10) **Metamorphic Water** ★

(11) **The Sound of Water** ★
Taku Satoh

(12) **Flat water**

(13) **Where does Tokyo's rain come from?** ★
Shinichi Takemura, Taku Satoh

extension of 21_21's branding. One of the cars is used to sell snacks and refreshments, while the other offers exhibition-related merchandise.

Ando's discreet building relies on a carefully modulated but enormous double-glazed wall to flood the exhibition area with natural light. The roof, welded together to seem like a single piece, is taken as a reference to Miyake's "one piece of cloth" approach to design, and allows the building to relate with delicacy to its immediate environment. Much of the building's internal space (finished in polished concrete) is below ground, and is reached by a dramatic staircase. One of the two wings is a café.

The opening temporary exhibition, curated by Naoto Fukasawa, presented chocolate creations by famous international designers.

Graphic and branding design: Taku Satoh Design Office
Creative direction and exhibition design: Naoto Fukasawa
Images: Courtesy of The Issey Miyake Foundation.
Photos: Masaya Yoshimura/Nacasa & Partners Inc.

Top, left: Graphics designed by Taku Satoh for a temporary exhibition on water and design.

Above, left: Nissan Cube cars were converted to serve as a food stall and merchandise store.

21_21 DESIGN SIGHT

"Ando's discreet building relies on a carefully modulated but enormous double-glazed wall to flood the exhibition area with natural light."

Top, left; bottom, left; and bottom, center: Further views of the restrained interior exhibition space.

Above: The website shares the meticulous attention to detail characteristic of the whole project.

Project
Museum of Croydon

Design
FAT (Fashion Architecture Taste)

Left: Whimsically stacked and vividly colored wall boxes were used for some of the small objects on display.

Above: Overview of the area dedicated to the early nineteenth century, showing the centrally installed "timeline" of urethane-sprayed furniture and guiding wall graphics.

Decidedly unfashionable Croydon, in south London's surburban hinterland, has been graced by an unusual museum, created to celebrate the lives of its citizens. FAT, a quirky architectural and design practice, was asked to refurbish the gallery and design an exhibition, housed in the old court room of an appropriately eccentric Victorian clock tower.

The objects on display were donated by the local community, and all tell a tale about the domestic and public lives of people in the area over the past couple of centuries. These are joined by a series of integrated audiovisual interactives intended to allow visitors to go deeper into the various stories that unfold.

The exhibits are contextualized by an unusual parallel display or "timeline." Furniture-derived objects, on plinths and with conspicuous design cues from the appropriate era, are coated in sprayed-on urethane. These create a "ghostly" atmosphere and historical context, while clearly demarcating themselves as support rather than objects on display. Distinctive wall graphics support the demarcation of different historic epochs.

The actual exhibition objects are all in display cases, either in glass at the center of the room or in closely hung wall-mounted frames. Studiously avoiding any

Top, right: Overview showing the unconventional display furniture and integrated interactives.

Right: Close-up showing the urethane "drapes" and glass display boxes.

Museum of Croydon

"The thing I love about the project is that it's a museum with nothing particularly valuable in it. It's everyday stuff, which makes it fascinating in a different way to most museums, which house 'special' and 'unusual' things. Trying to make sense of this, and to try to communicate the stories behind the objects was really the design challenge."

Sam Jacob, FAT

sense of being municipal, FAT's rich design also plays games with people's expectations of exhibition techniques, particularly Victorian ones.

"The thing I love about the project is that it's a museum with nothing particularly valuable in it. It's everyday stuff, which makes it fascinating in a different way to most museums which house 'special' and 'unusual' things," says Sam Jacob, one of FAT's founders. "Trying to make sense of this, and to try to communicate the stories behind the objects—the stories of the people who owned, or used the things on display—was really the design challenge."

Images: Courtesy of FAT

Left: Detail of one of the central glass display cabinets.

The concept was to present the furniture of Patricia Urquiola as industrial, as work in progress, rather than as art to be put on a plinth or pedestal. It was deliberately eschewing the craze for design art and the associated presentation.

Project
Dance n.2
Design
Patricia Urquiola and Martino Berghinz

Above: The lighting of the room was harsh and the bare floor accentuated the clinical, factory-like atmosphere of the show.

Right: Dance n.2 presented prototypes of Patricia Urquiola's furniture being carried around a blue painted factory-style production line.

Client
Stylepark

Location
Stylepark in Residence, Cologne

Dance n.2

> "Patricia Urquiola sheds light on her creative process in a very subjective manner and, not without a touch of self-irony, guides the observer's view to the origins of her creativity."
>
> **Christian Gärtner, Stylepark**

Cologne's annual furniture fair is an important fixture on the design calendar, and the fringe show staged by Stylepark has a good track record of showcasing the work of the more interesting designers. In 2007, Stylepark replaced its usual scattergun approach with a more curated show under the title Touchy-Feely, with the lion's share given over to a display of furniture by Patricia Urquiola, the Spanish designer regularly commissioned by the top-end Italian manufacturers.

The installation was designed by Urquiola and her studio partner Martino Berghinz, and presented her furniture designs in various states of completion or in prototype form, being carried around, suspended from a factory production line that went round in a circle in the otherwise bare room. This was a reworking on a larger and fuller scale of a similar installation they had created for the Arbitare II Tempo trade fair the previous year in Verona.

Berghinz explained that the concept was to present the furniture of Urquiola as industrial, as work in progress, rather than as art to be put on a plinth or pedestal. It was deliberately eschewing the craze for design art and the associated presentation.

"Patricia Urquiola sheds light on her creative process in a very subjective manner and, not without a touch of self-irony, guides the observer's view to the origins of her creativity. In this way we discover playfully how she comes up with her ideas. This poetic orchestration actually has little to do with a classic show of works," suggests Christian Gärtner of Stylepark.

But perhaps the installation's strength was that it was the very opposite of poetic. It was, however, reminiscent of the absurd, self-destructing installations of Dadaist sculptor Yves Tinguely. However, while Tinguely's noisy creations mocked the assembly line rigor and bathos of the technological modernity, Urquiola and Berghinz's intention was the opposite: to showcase the industrial process behind the furniture designs without recourse to too obvious a pedestal.

Photos: Stylepark/Constantin Meyer, Cologne

Far left: Martino Berghinz saw the production line itself as an industrial object of great beauty.

Left: The circular production line was at different heights, and carried the furniture designs Urquiola has designed for manufacturers such as Moroso, Kartell, and B&B Italia.

Top, right: The merry-go-round of fashionable furniture.

Project
GE/Fortune Innovation Conference

Design
Stone Yamashita Partners

WHAT BOX ARE
YOU IN—REALLY?

Are your core competencies
applicable to other products
and services?

Are there constraints limiting
the success of your products
and services?

Client
Fortune

Location
Lincoln Center, New York

"We designed and built a hands-on 'lab' where participants could try out new techniques, and could engage in conversation about what works and what does not."
Stone Yamashita Partners

Left: The "Innovation Laboratory" by Stone Yamashita and GE made much use of its dramatic location in the Allen Room at Jazz in the Lincoln Center, New York.

"Exemplary examples of breakthrough innovations were featured on a 30 foot by 8 foot wall of tear-sheet pads allowing attendees to tear off those they found interesting or relevant to their work."

GE/Fortune Innovation Conference

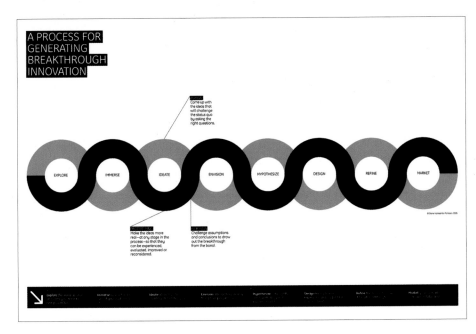

Innovation is a concept that can all too easily become abstract and drift into platitudes. So when San Francisco–based consultancy Stone Yamashita Partners (together with its client GE) was invited by Fortune to create an exhibit that would provide "an immersive experience of innovation," the firm decided it would build something that would make the concept of innovation something very real and tangible for those attending the Fortune Innovation Conference.

"We designed and built a hands-on 'lab' where participants could try out new techniques, and could engage in conversation about what works and what does not," explain the team behind the project. "The Fortune Innovation Conference attracted attendees that included CEOs, directors, and managers. Our objective was to communicate with attendees on several different levels, with the unifying theme being that the experience we created would be of value to anyone charged with driving change and innovation inside their organizations."

The exhibition's design did much to make the most of its enviable location in New York's Lincoln Center. But beneath the attractive aesthetics lay much work to develop effective content and interactives to engage with the theme of innovation.

Attendees were given various materials, including a workbook, which was styled as a guide to the "World's Largest Innovation Lab." While this assisted with the various interactive exercises, it was also intended as a self-sufficient account of the innovation process that attendees could take away with them and perhaps share with work colleagues who hadn't been to the show. In addition, some exemplary examples of breakthrough innovations were featured on a 30 foot by 8 foot (9 x 2.4 meter) wall of tear-sheet pads, allowing attendees to tear off those they found interesting or relevant to their work.

Creative directors/principals: Keith Yamashita, Susan Schuman, Lisa Maulhardt, Tom Andrews, Susana Rodriguez
Art directors: Vander McClain, Johnson Chow, Susana Rodriguez
Designers: Johnson Chow, Becky Hui, Julie Liu, Nicolas Maitret, Vander McClain
Illustrators: Nicolas Maitret, Becky Hui, Vander McClain
Production directors: Michelle Roach, Anne Bodel
Content strategists: Nicholas Anderson, Isobel Gotto, Jim Humes, Tom Raith
Structural designer: Johnson Chow
Photos: Gala Narezo

Top, left: The curved wall with giant tear-off pads with case studies of innovation in business that attendees could rip off and take away with them.

Bottom, left: Close-up of the wall.

Top, center: Example of the didactic graphics at the exhibition.

Top, right: The graphics in situ.

Above: Overview of the exhibition in full swing, showing the many different kinds of interaction intended for its business audience.

Right: Close-up of one of the business interactives.

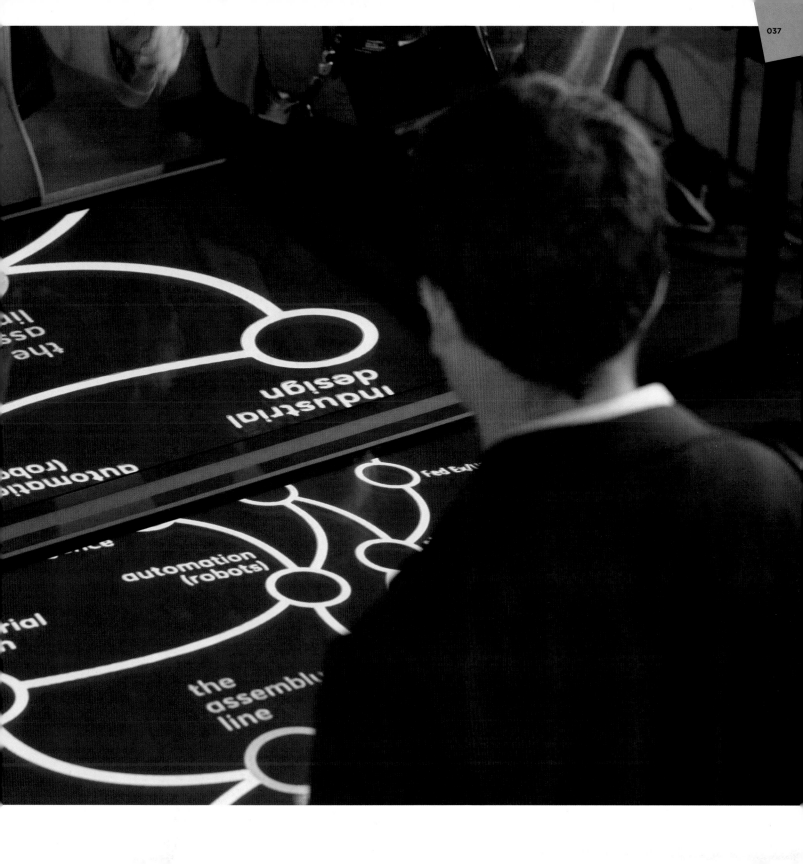

Project
Installations for the Goodwood Festival of Speed

Design
Gerry Judah

Client
Goodwood Festival of Speed together with Rolls-Royce, Honda, and Toyota

Location
Goodwood

"I view it as installation art... It is important to design things from the perspective of a view on the ground, rather than as a plan on paper."

Gerry Judah

The Goodwood Festival of Speed, an annual celebration of classic racing cars, has rapidly established itself as a major event, and every year the dramatic centerpieces commissioned from sculptor designer Gerry Judah manage to be one of the highlights. A different automobile manufacturer is honored every year, and it is that marque's cars that are taken as the starting point for Judah's creation, which has to function as a focal center of attention for the show and its defining image.

"I know the space and have a feeling for what will work," says Judah. "It has to give the feeling of a different space every year. It's the central display, but has to stand out year after year, and be exuberant and entertaining."

Left and right: Gerry Judah's 2004 Goodwood Festival of Speed centerpiece featuring Rolls-Royce automobiles and airplanes mounted on enormous winged structures in front of Goodwood House.

"My approach is that of sculpture, I view it as installation art—that's more important than the car. The first thing I want is for people to see it and go 'wow!' That's the whole point of it—to provide an immediate thrill," he adds. Earlier in his career, Judah worked in theater and movie set design, a background he feels has been very helpful. "I understand showbiz," he says simply.

Working with Toyota for the stand for the 2007 show was a difficult experience because the Japanese manufacturer had strong ideas of its own which were largely derived from motor show designs. "I have a totally different way of working," says Judah. "It is important to design things from the perspective of a view on the ground, rather than as a plan on paper."

Structural engineers: Atelier One (Rolls-Royce), NRM Bobrowski (Honda and Toyota)
Photos: David Barbour

Left: Detail of the Rolls-Royce installation of 2004.

Top, right and right: Honda was the manufacturer celebrated in the centerpiece to the 2005 Goodwood Festival of Speed.

Installations for the Goodwood Festival of Speed

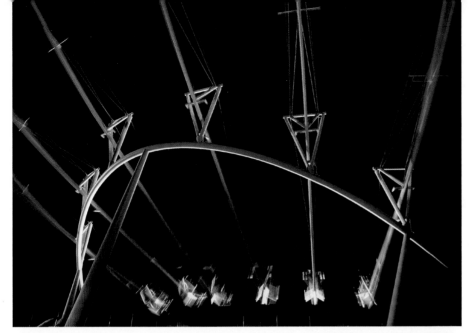

"The first thing I want is for people to see it and go 'wow!' That's the whole point of it—to provide an immediate thrill."

Gerry Judah

Above: Detail of the Honda installation of 2005.

Installations for the Goodwood Festival of Speed

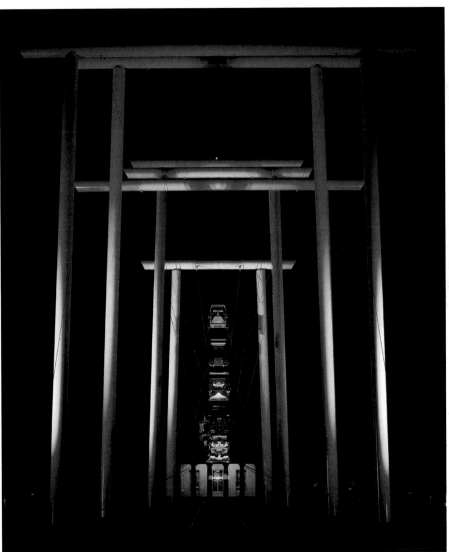

Above, left and right: The 131 foot (40 meter) high structure showcasing Toyota for the 2007 Goodwood Festival of Speed was inspired by Japanese "torii" gates and featured racing cars held in intricate and dynamic suspension.

Above: Graphic welcoming visitors to the show.

Right: The entire show was centered on Pentagram's reformulation of Katharine Gates' erotic roadmap.

Client
Museum of Sex

Location
New York

> "The *New York Times* described the design as akin to 'a torn fishnet stocking pulled over shapeless flesh,'... We took it as a compliment."
>
> **Michael Bierut, Pentagram**

New York's Museum of Sex decided to stage a show exploring the many different avenues that sexual dissidence and experimentation can take. Its starting point was a road map of deviancy, devised by Katherine Gates, author of *Deviant Desires* and cocurator of the exhibition.

The idea of the show was, quite literally, to present "a journey through the erotic imagination." For Pentagram, this translated into an intriguing brief, approached with the clarity if not purity of Harry Beck's seminal map of the London Underground.

"Our design of Kink began with our fascination with the amazing map that Katharine Gates had developed as part of her scholarly work on the subject," says Pentagram partner Michael Bierut. "We felt that if we could give it a compelling treatment, that would inform the rest of the exhibition. Obviously, this is what happened, from typography to color scheme to the overall 'more is more' sensibility. The critic in the *New York Times* described the design as akin to 'a torn fishnet stocking pulled over shapeless flesh,' which I think he intended as a criticism. We took it as a compliment."

Top, right: Different stations around the show were dedicated to particular fetishes.

Above, right: Interactivity doesn't need to be technological.

Kink: Geography of the Erotic Imagination

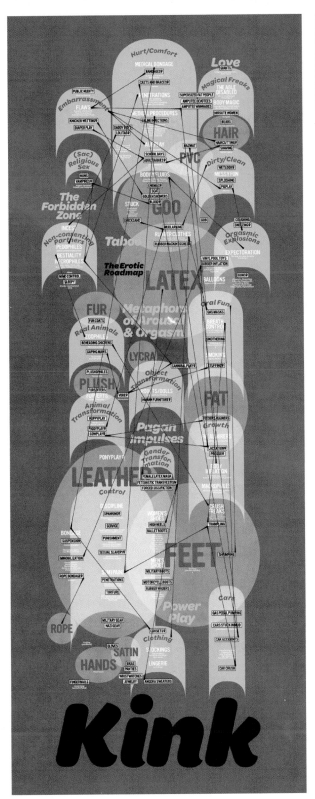

Different stops along the way allowed visitors to engage with various forms of eroticism. "Our focus was on keeping the dense and 'kinky' information accessible and approachable," adds project designer Jennifer Kinon. "Katharine felt a big responsibility to the people she was profiling and we felt a big responsibility to her. The idea was to make clear through exhibit design that kinks are most often just very playful and personal."

Lead designers: Michael Bierut, Jennifer Kinon
Photos: Benya Hegenbarth

Left: Pentagram's formulation of Katharine Gates' erotic roadmap in full.

Top: The show relied heavily on Pentagram's graphic treatment and eye-watering selection of pinks.

Project
Musée du quai Branly

Design
Ateliers Jean Nouvel

Client
**Etablissement Public du
Musée du quai Branly**

Location
Paris

"Away, then, with the structures, mechanical systems, with curtain walls, with emergency staircases, parapets, false ceilings, projectors, pedestals, show-cases. This is an asylum for censored and cast-off objects, whether they come from Australia or the Americas."
Jean Nouvel

Left: The colorful rear façade of Jean Nouvel's Musée du quai Branly, overlooking the landscaped gardens, announces its eccentricity to the world.

Musée du quai Branly

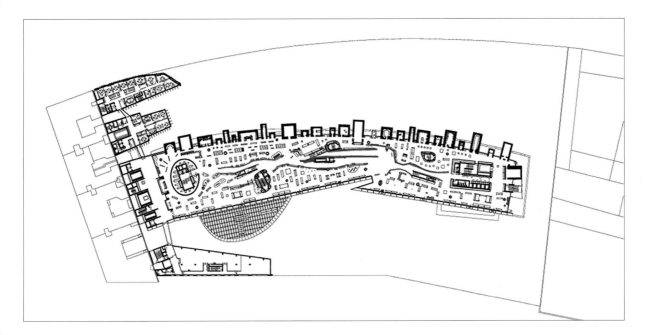

"A museum about the other can't be a museum like the others," says architect Jean Nouvel about the Musée du quai Branly. A recent addition to the "grand projets" of Paris thanks to the support of then President Jacques Chirac, the museum was built to house and unify the ethnographic collections of the city.

While acknowledging that a collection of non-European artifacts such as these "beg collective questions that go beyond the architectural," Nouvel's eccentric and controversial response is as much about museology as it is about design.

Nouvel casts away the conventional bland white space with objects contextualized with graphics and labels, presenting a controversial, highly colored aesthetic experience in its place. A dense, forest-like space (or jungle, to its detractors) is created rather than the usual neutral, discreet shell. "Allusion rather than illusion," says Nouvel, junking the standard apparatus of the museum to announce that "viewing and inquiry, contemplation and information, admiration and learning—these are two distinct things."

Nouvel says he wanted to move away from Western rationalism "to give the objects a home in which they could be by themselves and conduct their own dialogue" or "lead their own lives." The result, he says, is "an asylum for objects that have been censured and misunderstood, whether they come from Australia or the Americas."

The heart of the museum is a single, irregularly shaped exhibition space over 656 feet (200 meters) long, reached by walking up a dimly lit circular ramp. This main space has two "snakes" (a pale leather clad structure housing seating and information) meandering through it. Glass display cases are constructed so as to seem to have no edges, and the idea is for objects to simply float in front of the viewer at eye level. Information is removed to some considerable distance from the artifact, so as not to interfere with the primary interaction with the exhibit.

Whether this is condescending, patronizing, or even colonial, as some critics have claimed, or a genuinely radical architectural and philosophical attempt to find a solution for presenting increasingly contested and controversial objects, is for each visitor to decide. At the very least, it does manage, both visually and conceptually, to be a museum apart.

Photos: Musee du quai Branly © 2007. Nicholas Borel/ Scala, Florence

Left: The dense, atmospheric main exhibition space, showing the "snakes," the pale leather covered structures that combine seating and display information.

Top: Plan of the main exhibition floor, showing the nonrectilinear use of space and the manner in which the "snakes" cross it.

"Allusion rather than illusion, viewing and inquiry, contemplation and information, admiration and learning—these are two distinct things."

Jean Nouvel

Above: View of the central glass structure housing the reserves and showing the louvered glass exterior.

Right: The ramp circles a display of musical instruments from the museum's reserves encased by 52 ½ foot (16 meter) high glass.

den 11. time

Project
CPH Experiments

Design
Bjarke Ingels Group (BIG)

CPH Experiments

Client
**Storefront for Art
and Architecture**

Location
New York

When Bjarke Ingels Group (BIG), a young Danish architectural practice, was asked to put on an exhibition of its work at the Storefront for Art and Architecture in New York, it decided to showcase five of its public housing projects with a display of models. But with a difference—one of the models was constructed out of Lego bricks, quite appropriate as Lego was BIG's client for the building in question.

"When we entered the competition to build the Lego building, we went to the Lego website and downloaded a program that allows you to design something in Lego. We did the plans, sent it off, and they sent us the pieces," explains Kai-Uwe Bergmann. "That was in 1:500 scale and we won the competition. But when it came to the show we thought why not make it 1:50 scale, to match the scale of the famous Lego figures."

Far left: Overview of the model of the Lego building made from Lego bricks that was the centerpiece of the CPH Experiments exhibition.

Left: Detail of the Lego model, showing 1:50 scale standard Lego figures and the internal lighting.

Lego was happy to be involved, and duly sent the 250,000 pieces, which were then assembled by student helpers, the whole process being recorded on a video posted on YouTube. It was then shipped to New York, with the other models, to star in the show.

"We tried to make the exhibition an intuitive experience," says Bergmann. "The five models were to different scales, placed obliquely, and each accompanied by an abstract graphic on the wall. There were also three screens (supplied by Bang & Olufsen) showing animations, allowing the visitor to understand the projects from different perspectives. Detailed project descriptions were printed on newsprint [designed in-house by BIG] and available at the door for those wanting more information."

BIG always lights its models internally, but the Lego model required a bit of extra external lighting. For Storefront's famous Stephen Holl–designed frontage, BIG decided simply to paint one panel green and mark it the "Big Entrance" and another red as the "Big Exit," injecting more humor into proceedings as well as helping to articulate the path through the tight 262 ½ square foot (80 square meter) space.

"Architectural models usually only appeal to architecture students and professionals, but this brought in a broad crowd, from kids dragging in their parents, to Lego enthusiasts, and beyond," says Bergmann.

"We are really keen to use exhibitions to communicate our work to reach a broader audience. As a teacher told me, when, as an architect, you build something, only a few people will experience it physically. For most it will just be a picture in a book or magazine. With an exhibition, you get somewhere in between."

Lead designers: Bjarke Ingels, Kai-Uwe Bergmann
Budget: $90,000 US
Photos: © BIG

Top, right: Punning entrance to the exhibition, showing the newsprint guide and exterior of the Storefront.

Top, far right: Final stages of construction and installation of the model. The model was lit both internally and externally, here to give the impression of what the building would look like at night.

Bottom, right: Poster created by BIG for the exhibition.

Bottom, far right: Another view of the installation of the model, showing the other exhibits in the background.

"When, as an architect, you build something, only a few people will experience it physically. For most it will just be a picture in a book or magazine. With an exhibition, you get somewhere in between."
Kai-Uwe Bergmann, BIG

Storefront for Art and Architecture
97 KENMARE STREET NEW YORK NY 10012 TEL 212 431 5795
www.storefrontnews.org

CPH EXPERIMENTS

5 NEW ARCHITECTURAL SPECIES FROM THE DANISH WELFARE STATE BY BJARKE INGELS GROUP

2 OCTOBER - 24 NOVEMBER 2007 TUESDAY - SATURDAY 12AM - 7.30PM

"There is no hierarchical relationship between architecture and exhibition design."

Professor H.G. Merz, HG Merz

Project
Mercedes-Benz Museum

Exhibition Design
HG Merz

Client
DaimlerChrysler

Above: The view of UNStudio's Mercedes-Benz Museum that greets drivers at night.

Bottom, right: Display of the iconic Gullwing Mercedes, showing the stark concrete interior and large-scale graphics.

Top, right: Detail showing the circular walkways that loop around the space.

The extraordinary sight that greets people driving by or visiting the Mercedes-Benz Museum is the result of the unlikely but close collaboration between German exhibition design group HG Merz and UNStudio, an off-beat architectural practice based in the Netherlands.

HG Merz had been retained right at the very start of the project, before even the decision to commission a new building was taken. The firm drew up a master plan for the exhibition and took a curatorial role, selecting objects from the car maker's extensive collection. HG Merz then worked with the board of DaimlerChrysler (now Daimler) to create the specifications for a competition for a new building.

HG Merz developed the idea of a two-part collection: Legends would be a permanent collection of significant Mercedes models from the company's history, and these would be accompanied by "collections" or "deposits," which are, in essence, curated temporary selections from Mercedes' extensive collection of cars, commercial vehicles, and automobilia.

UNStudio beat nine other entrants to win the architecture competition, and used HG Merz's concept to develop a highly unusual building based on the notion of interlocking trefoil shapes, in which the visitor experience is one of constant interlooping. This dynamism, naturally, is very appropriate for the automotive subjects of the display.

The materials of the build and installation, whether metal or concrete, never stray far from the silver that has become a notable part of the design of the Mercedes since the 1930s. The actual building is self evidently a technological tour de force, again feeding into the brand values that Mercedes-Benz wishes to present to the world.

"There is no hierarchical relationship between architecture and exhibition design but a perfectly matched quality," says Professor H.G. Merz. "The concept of the content was mutually adjusted and led to a harmonious cooperation between the architects and the museum design team." His company was also responsible for all the graphics and information systems at the Mercedes-Benz Museum.

Images: Courtesy of Daimler

Top, left: The first of the Legend rooms, featuring the first cars by Gottlieb Daimler and Karl Benz, designed in 1886.

Top, right: The continuous curve architecture morphs into banking for a high-level display of Silver Arrow world speed record cars.

Bottom, right: Routing through the Mercedes-Benz Museum, as plotted by its architects, Ben van Berkel and Caroline Bos of UNStudio.

Far right: The museum exterior during the day.

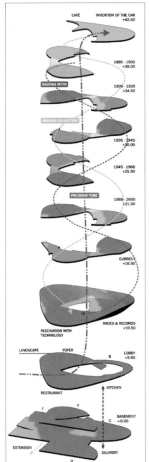

CAFÉ   INVENTION OF THE CAR
+42.50

1886 - 1900
+39.00

ROUTING MYTH

1900 - 1926
+34.50

ROUTING COLLECTION

1926 - 1945
+30.00

1945 - 1968
+25.50

PRE-SHOW TUBE

1968 - 2000
+21.00

CURRENT
+16.50

FASCINATION WITH   RACES & RECORDS
TECHNOLOGY   +10.50

LANDSCAPE   FOYER   LOBBY
+5.60

RESTAURANT   KITCHEN

BASEMENT
+0.00

EXTENSION   DELIVERY

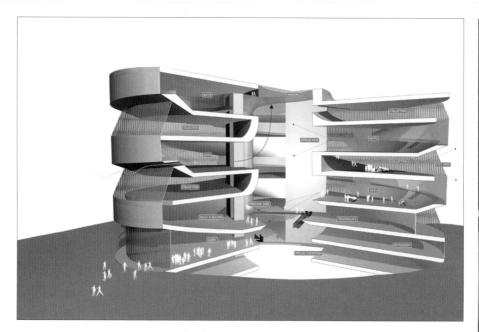

Top: Cross section by UNStudio of the museum.

Above: Concept cars are placed on giant mushroom-shaped plinths.

Right: The oldest extant Mercedes, built in 1902, has its place of honor marked by a special lighting installation above it.

Rip Curl Canyon

Left: View of the Rip Curl Canyon installation from outside the Rice Gallery at night.

Above: A visitor walking on top of the bonded cardboard surface of the Rip Curl Canyon. Both photos www.nashbaker.com

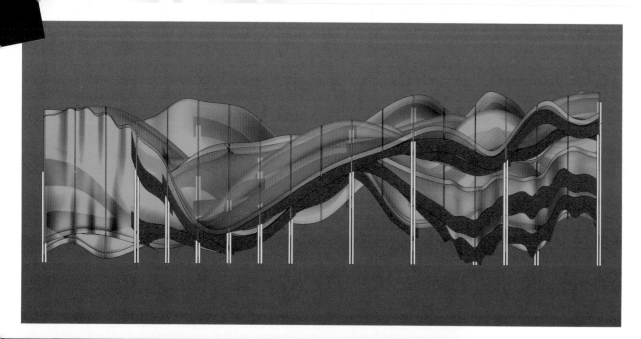

Crowding a gallery with two long ribbons of cut, bonded cardboard, Ball-Nogues created an environment that intrigued visitors while inviting them to take part, climb, and explore the complex spatial forms.

"We approached the aesthetics of the installation as though it were a shifting land or water form to be traversed by visitors to the gallery," says Benjamin Ball, one half of Ball-Nogues. "It was as though there were tectonic shifts moving through a three-dimensional Grant Wood painting."

The installation was commissioned to accompany a concurrent exhibition of modern American landscape painting at The Museum of Fine Arts in Houston. "Exhibition design assumes specific purposes: advertising, communication, display," says Ball. "Rip Curl Canyon was built in a gallery so its purpose or intent was entirely up to us as the makers. We come from a design background; it is customary for us to imagine projects with a program, so we chose to extend the relaxed social space of the Rice University campus into the gallery, letting the installation become a space of exploration and play for the visitor." And as visitors clambered over the surface, they left their mark in the form of pathways created where the cardboard had become compressed.

Top, left: A digital image generated during the design gestation of the Rip Curl Canyon.

Left: Detail showing the 4 x 2 inch (10 x 5 centimeter) plywood support structure. Photo www.nashbaker.com

Rip Curl Canyon

"We approached the aesthetics of the installation as though it were a shifting land or water form to be traversed by visitors to the gallery. It was as though there were tectonic shifts moving through a three-dimensional Grant Wood painting."

Benjamin Ball, Ball-Nogues

Also apparent, beneath the surface attraction of the Rip Curl Canyon, is a tension between the digital conception and the craft of modeling of the final result. The two designers spent over half a year translating computer simulations into 4,000 precision cuttings of cardboard, which were then painstakingly assembled on-site atop an elevated, plywood frame to create this mythical, artificial landscape.

The Rip Curl Canyon could just as easily be termed craft, exhibition design, or art, though the emerging category of installation architecture is the one most frequently adopted. Both Ball and Gastón Nogues trained as architects and worked for Frank Gehry, but their distinctive approach is also the result of Ball's experience in movie set design and Nogues' as a product designer.

Top, left: The central "canyon" of the installation.

Left: Side view of the installation. Both photos www.nashbaker.com

Above: The "grid" designed by Experimental Jetset transforms the exhibition space displaying Johannes Schwartz's photography of staircases, itself about the ambiguity of space.

Right: The "grid" is at an angle to the existing architecture to create moments of dislocation, and is made of wood.

Stair/Stare

> "We were looking at the floor drawings of Marres, and suddenly asked ourselves what would happen if we would overlay these drawings with themselves. In other words, if we took the drawings, tilted them a bit, and put them on top of the original drawings… what would this mean if this would be translated to the actual space?"
>
> **Experimental Jetset**

Ambiguity is one of the primary themes running through the photographs of Johannes Schwartz. It is something apparent in a series of photographs of staircases in various stages of completion or dilapidation taken in Egypt, which were assembled for an exhibition entitled Stair/Stare, at the Centrum voor contemporaine cultuur in Maastricht. Schwartz invited graphic designers Experimental Jetset and architect/exhibition designer Herman Verkerk to collaborate on the show. Fittingly, each adopted ambiguous roles. "It was a very unpredictable cooperation, more of a free-form association," says Schwartz. "It now looks very calculated, but it was actually very spontaneous."

Verkerk contributed a small installation in the stairwell, playing on the ideas of steps with Lego pieces. Experimental Jetset, on the other hand, translated the "grid" mindset of graphic design into a novel three-dimensional structure that made something completely new out of the classical exhibition area of the Marres. It is, in the words of Schwartz, "a space within a space," and manages to create a visual backdrop and unity to the space, while undermining it subtly in a way that ties up with the photographs on display.

Experimental Jetset hit upon the idea after playing around with ground plans of the exhibition space.

"We abstracted the walls of Marres into a sort of three-dimensional 'line drawing' and placed this construction back in the space itself. We tilted it a little bit, to make this more visible and also decided that the construction should be black, to refer to the idea of a line drawing," explains Experimental Jetset. "It is almost a 'ghost image' of Marres itself, appearing as though it runs right through walls, just as ghosts walk through walls in movies."

Photos: Johannes Schwartz

Far left: Herman Verkerk's installation on the Marres staircase, made of Lego pieces.

Bottom, left: A maquette made by Experimental Jetset to persuade the management of the Marres gallery to accept these transformations of the space. Courtesy of Experimental Jetset.

Top, left: One of the primary exhibits at the show: a photograph by Johannes Schwartz of a stairwell at a construction site in Egypt.

Top, right: The more colorful intervention on the staircase.

Above: The gallery's own stairwell transformed for Stair/Stare.

Right: The "grid" extended to the exterior of the building.

"It was a very unpredictable cooperation, more of a free-form association. It now looks very calculated, but it was actually very spontaneous."
Johannes Schwartz

Right: Image showing the disorienting relation of the exhibition installation and the photography.

Wallpaper*

EcoEdit

If you want to keep up to speed with all that's new and nifty at Salone del Mobile, log onto www.wallpaper.com and visit the Wallpaper* Global EcoEdit exhibition:

- Wallpaper's first ever online curated gallery showcasing the best-looking eco-friendly design, architecture and fashion from around the world
- Daily news reports from the world's biggest furniture fair
- The latest trends, identified and thoroughly investigated
- Unique collaborations with leading designers, including Studio Job, Jaime Hayon, Pierre Paulin, Autoban and Peter Marigold
- Daily weblogs from the Wallpaper* team
- An exclusive and indispensable guide to Milan's shopping

At www.wallpaper.com

Project
EcoEdit

Design
Wallpaper*

Client
Self-initiated

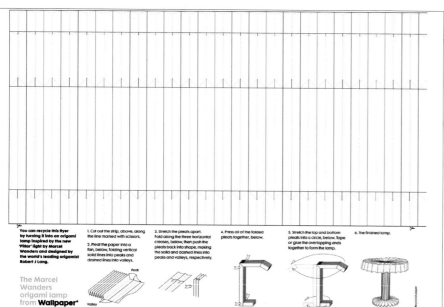

You can recycle this flyer by turning it into an origami lamp inspired by the new 'Pillar' light by Marcel Wanders and designed by the world's leading origamist Robert J Lang.

1. Cut out the strip, above, along the line marked with scissors.

2. Pleat the paper into a fan, below, folding vertical solid lines into peaks and dashed lines into valleys.

3. Stretch the pleats apart. Fold along the three horizontal creases, below, then push the pleats back into shape, making the solid and dashed lines into peaks and valleys, respectively.

4. Press all of the folded pleats together, below.

5. Stretch the top and bottom pleats into a circle, below. Tape or glue the overlapping ends together to form the lamp.

6. The finished lamp.

The Marcel Wanders origami lamp from **Wallpaper***

Location
**Online at www.wallpaper.
com/ecoedit/ecoedit.html**

"Rather than flying the designs around the world, or sending photographers off to shoot them, we have chosen to represent them with stunning illustrations instead."
*Wallpaper**

Top and bottom, far left: The flyer for the online show that was distributed around Milan included a do-it-yourself lamp designed by Marcel Wanders and origamist Robert L. Lang.

Left: Hort's illustration of organic tea. All illustrations © Hort.

More usually associated with conspicuous over-consumption, glossy style magazine *Wallpaper** decided to mark its presence at the 2007 Salone del Mobile (Milan Furniture Fair) by swapping the comforts and carbon excesses of a first-class flight for the more subtle charms of a website. Entitled EcoEdit, and curated internally, a total of 101 ecological yet beautifully designed products were featured. As the world's major design event, the Milan Furniture Fair always features exhibition displays created by top designers, and achieving standout is a considerable challenge.

"Rather than flying the designs around the world, or sending photographers off to shoot them, we have chosen to represent them with stunning illustrations instead," the magazine announced. And the illustrations, by German group Hort, responded with a distinctly unglossy and ethereal approach to the products, drawing out their qualities without recourse to the standard, overused, visual language of environmentalism. Instead of predictable ochers and greens, the design uses blacks and pastels to make its point. Only the opening logo references existing iconography, with a nod in the direction of the standard recycling logo.

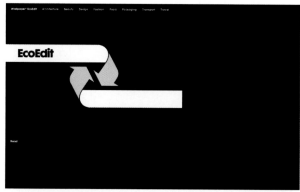

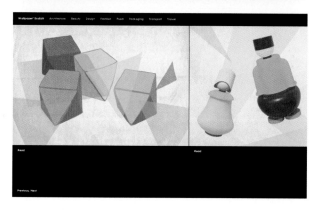

Top, left: Hort's illustration of Pangea Organics beauty products.

Center, right: Homepage of *Wallpaper**'s EcoEdit.**

Bottom, right: Part of the website that looks at design objects. Text has to be clicked on to become fully visible.

"The innovative and environmentally friendly projects chosen were drawn from the fields of architecture, beauty, fashion, food, packaging, product design, transport, and travel."

The innovative and environmentally friendly projects chosen were drawn from the fields of architecture, beauty, fashion, food, packaging, product design, transport, and travel.

The magazine was also happy to announce that a "promotional flyer, produced in origami paper, will be distributed around Milan by beautiful young *Wallpaper**-branded cyclists directing people to the exhibition." When folded, this became a miniature version of a Marcel Wanders' folding lampshade commissioned to coincide with the show.

Illustrator: Hort
Designer: Andrew McManus

Left: Hort's illustration of eco jewelery.

"We wanted the Dreamspace to be a place that let visitors see the way Boeing thinks."
Adam Evans, FITCHLive

Project
Dreamspace

Design
FITCHLive

Client
Boeing

Dreamspace

Farnborough International Air Show

Left: The Dreamspace from outside.

Above: Entering the Dreamspace, the visitor walked along a series of models of Boeing aircraft that appeared to be taking off.

"Air shows are extremely hectic and loud environments. We wanted to create an environment that was calm, relaxed, and inviting for guests and the public to spend time in talking with Boeing and discovering the new developments at their own pace."

Adam Evans, FITCHLive

Top, left: This large interactive screen could be used by visitors to specify or conduct virtual tours of the new aircraft.

Bottom, right: Detail of the distinctive yet soothing lighting of the Dreamspace.

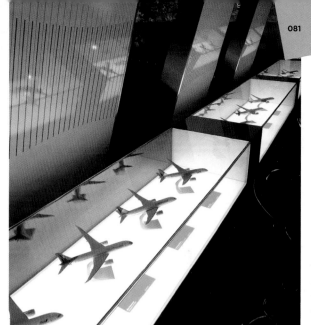

For the Farnborough International Air Show in 2006, FITCHLive and its longstanding client Boeing had a considerable challenge. Arch-competitor Airbus had literally stolen the show by bringing along its new supersize A380 passenger jet—whatever Boeing had to say to potential clients and the general public was going to be, quite literally, in the shade of this behemoth.

Rather than compete by shouting loudly, FITCHLive decided to create a relaxing and inviting space for Boeing to communicate the environmental advances it was making with its new 787 Dreamliner and 747-8 aircraft. "We wanted the Dreamspace to be a place that let visitors see the way Boeing thinks. Although the huge A380 was parked outside, we felt that creating a well-designed, calm, listening environment that allowed visitors to talk to Boeing and find out what they wanted to know was both memorable and 'felt Boeing,'" says Adam Evans of FITCHLive. The new Dreamliner aircraft presents a new, more passenger-friendly environment, and the Dreamspace, which co-opted its branding, had to present those same values.

A large interactive screen was placed at the center of the Dreamspace which allowed hosts and users to choose the content they wanted to see. "With guests all having their own individual agendas and time restraints, Boeing staff were able to tailor presentations according to individual requests and relevance," explains Evans.

The area dedicated to the 747-8 aircraft featured a "champagne wall" as a way of bringing to life Boeing's strapline "What do you do when the price of fuel is the same as champagne? Sip it." This was a full-length wall that bubbled away behind copy detailing the 747-8's efficiency comparisons.

The nature of the show, as well as the long-standing relationship between designer and client, meant that the project was deeply collaborative. FITCHLive was able to draw on animations created by Boeing's in-house team as well as their skills in transporting and installing a section of the 787 fuselage, the interior of which formed an intriguing part of the Dreamspace.

Images: Courtesy of FitchLive

Top, center: The Dreamspace used subtle lighting and reflective surfaces to create a soothing and ethereal environment.

Top, right: The "champagne wall" that presented the energy efficiencies of the new 747-8 aircraft with the strapline: "What do you do when the price of fuel is the same as champagne? Sip it."

Top, far right: A display of models of the new Dreamliner in the liveries of the different airlines that had purchased the jet.

Project
Bob Dylan's American Journey, 1956–1966

Design
Wonder Mine

Top: Black leather was used for the display covering the period when Dylan decided to go electric and become a rock star.

Above: The unconventional use of concrete was intended to give an urban flavor to the display of materials relating to this period of Dylan's career.

Right: Partially transparent photomural wall with an image of Bob Dylan and his lyrics, designed to create an inviting start to the show.

Bob Dylan's American Journey, 1956–1966

Client
Experience Music Project

Location
Traveling exhibition

Replacing a forbidding wall, a large photomural of Bob Dylan draws visitors into a carefully thought out traveling exhibition, giving a sense of immersion in the life of the folk music legend.

The approach of Ken Burns, the exhibition's designer, was inspired by a bag of striking red-orange iron ore that the exhibition's curator, Jasen Emmens, brought back from Bob Dylan's hometown of Hibbing, Minnesota. The decision was then made to use unusual but evocative and relevant materials to subtly engage the viewer.

"Some 1,500 pounds of actual iron ore from Hibbing was used as an introductory backdrop for the story of Dylan's mining town origins," says Burns. "Choosing to use the iron ore led to using a brick-red wall color and a decision to use other natural, tactile materials. I chose a combination of yellow suede and concrete surfaces to evoke an urban environment and the 'citybilly' character of the Urban Folk Revival movement that Dylan was a big part of. Black leather was used to mark the point in Dylan's career where he dons a leather jacket, plugs in, and becomes a rock star." Silk screening and flatbed printing allowed the use of these unconventional materials.

Top, right: The central row of booths from the outside.

Right: Graphics were printed on suede to give a "citybilly" character to the show.

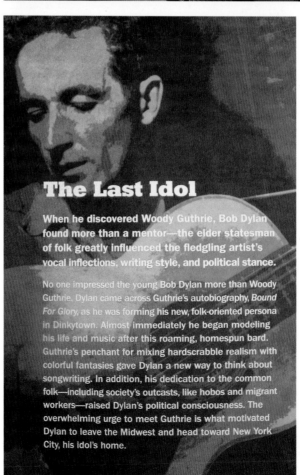

The Last Idol

When he discovered Woody Guthrie, Bob Dylan found more than a mentor—the elder statesman of folk greatly influenced the fledgling artist's vocal inflections, writing style, and political stance.

No one impressed the young Bob Dylan more than Woody Guthrie. Dylan came across Guthrie's autobiography, *Bound For Glory*, as he was forming his new, folk-oriented persona in Dinkytown. Almost immediately he began modeling his life and music after this roaming, homespun bard. Guthrie's penchant for mixing hardscrabble realism with colorful fantasies gave Dylan a new way to think about songwriting. In addition, his dedication to the common folk—including society's outcasts, like hobos and migrant workers—raised Dylan's political consciousness. The overwhelming urge to meet Guthrie is what motivated Dylan to leave the Midwest and head toward New York City, his idol's home.

Bob Dylan's American Journey, 1956–1966

"The approach was inspired by a bag of striking red-orange iron ore brought back from Bob Dylan's hometown of Hibbing, Minnesota. The decision was then made to use unusual but evocative and relevant materials to subtly engage the viewer."

Rare footage and recordings were also an essential part of the 2,500 square foot (762 square meter) exhibition. The materials used to construct the various sections had to allow visitors in small groups to be able to engage with the music and film, while controlling sound levels so as not to impose on other parts of the show with their own music. Despite these discreet sonic booths, the openness and transparency of much of the exhibition display furniture draws visitors—primarily school groups—through the show.

Lead designers: Ken Burns, Sandy Owen
Budget: $900,000 US
Photos: Lara Swimmer

Top, right: Detail showing the rock wall inspired by and using iron ore from Dylan's mining hometown of Hibbing.

Right: One of the booths, showing rare film footage of Dylan.

"The unique result was a strikingly decked out tram, which functioned as an exhibition space hosting events such as movies, readings, and autographing sessions."

PROJECT PUMA Charity Tram

DESIGN GBH Design

PUMA Charity Tram

Client:
PUMA International

Location:
Berlin

Left: A Berlin tram covered in distinctive graphics by GBH Design. All photos by Nick Gutteridge.

Above, center: Detail of a tram interior showing the interactives, which provided more information about African soccer.

Above, right: The trams were fully functioning and traveled around Berlin for the length of the FIFA World Cup competition.

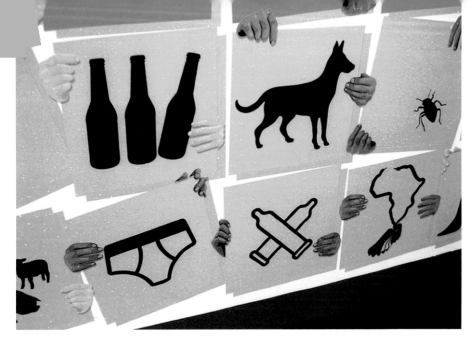

"Creating a store on a tram, disguised as an African Charity awareness scheme, under the gaze of the German Transport Police, was one of the most bizarre exercises in problem solving and people politics we have ever undertaken."

Peter Hale, GBH Design

"The brief for the PUMA Charity Tram was interesting and very complicated," says Peter Hale of London–based GBH Design. "We were asked to transform a functioning Berlin tram into a PUMA soccer-themed store and recreation space during the four weeks of the 2006 FIFA World Cup. But as PUMA is also the leading sponsor of the African teams and the charity United For Africa, the tram also represented an opportunity to raise awareness and donations for the cause. So how do you bring all those requirements together in a way that looks simple, striking, and satisfies one of the most stringent transport codes in the world?"

The unique result was a strikingly decked out tram, which functioned as an exhibition space hosting events such as movies, readings, and autographing sessions. Interactives showcased African soccer and explained the aims of the charity. The tram ran along a dedicated route from midday to midnight, and while jumping on board cost nothing, passengers were encouraged to make donations to the cause. Stops included some of the most prominent places in the city, but whether it stopped at all depended on the nature of the event being hosted that day.

One of the carriages, termed a "retail entertainment tram," was converted into a store selling merchandise from the PUMA Charity Collection. Part of the profits went to United for Africa, an umbrella organization of 30 different charities. A CD and book were also sold as part of the initiative.

Designers: Peter Hale, Ian McLean, Mark Wheatcroft, Richard Coward
Technical designer: Ines Teichert
Shopfitters: Markstrahler+Barth
Illustrator: Benedict Campbell

Top: Close-up of the exterior graphics on the tram.

Bottom, right: Entrance to one of the trams, showing the slogan "Get on it" used for the initiative.

Top, center: The branding was inspired by transport maps.

Top, right: Examples of the merchandise sold in the trams, showing the project branding and transparent pricing and donations.

Get on it™

UNITED FOR AFRICA/PUMA TRAM EXPERIENCE

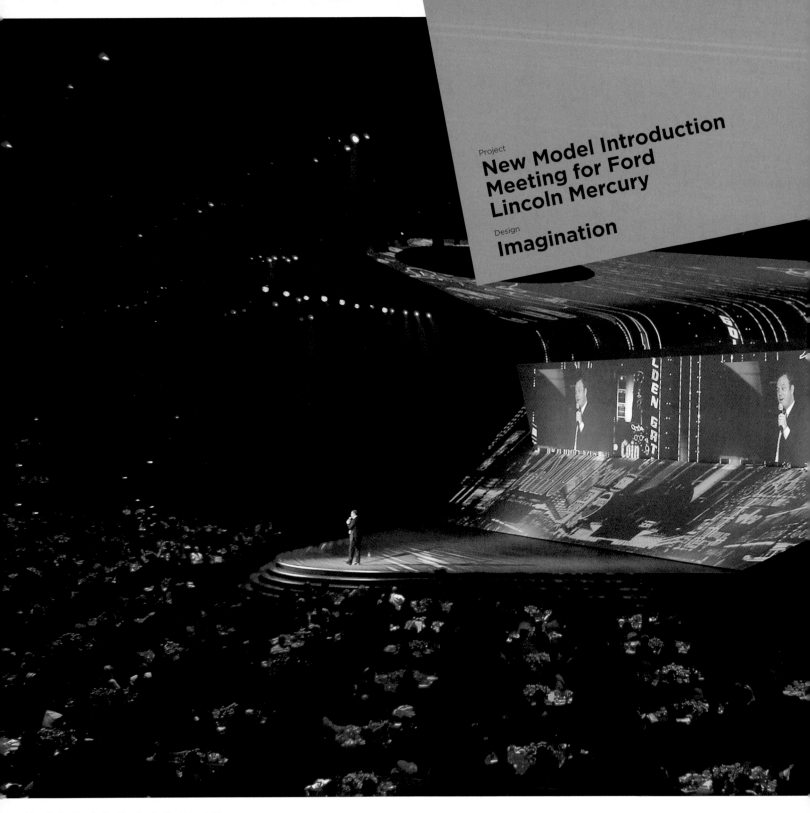

Project
New Model Introduction Meeting for Ford Lincoln Mercury

Design
Imagination

Client
Ford Motor Company

Location
Mandalay Bay Arena, Las Vegas

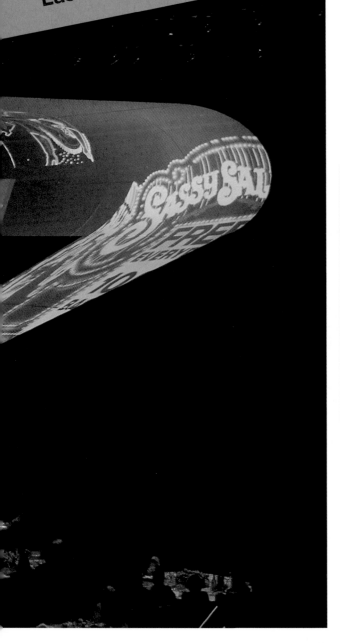

Left: Overview of main stage area and screen during post-gala concert.

Above: Close-up of the main stage area, showing the smaller pop-up screen used for animated imagery.

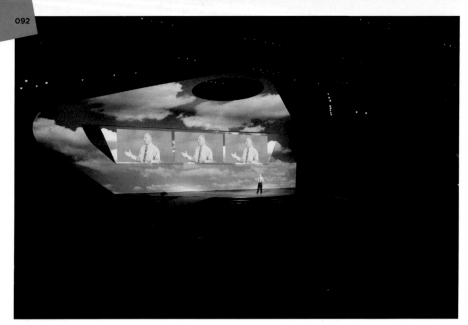

"This was a space that worked equally well for a car show, business meeting, and a rock concert. It's all about bringing in theatrical techniques to communicate and create emotional impact."

Martin Grant, Imagination

The Ford Motor Company, a long-term client of Imagination, wanted an event to present new models from its Ford, Lincoln, and Mercury marques to the national network of dealers, and draw a line under recent well-publicized difficulties, while at the same time leaving the attendees uplifted and impressed by the spectacle. Projections on a giant screen, 120 feet (36.5 meters) across, 40 feet (12.1 meters) high, and 60 feet (18.2 meters) front to back, in the form of a wave about to break, answered Ford's desire for a bold brand experience to reinvigorate its dealers. "Ford wanted something completely different, something that hadn't been done before. This was a dramatic, awe-inspiring shape, that had metaphorical significance, but also had practical benefits," says Imagination's Martin Grant.

Some 15 digital projectors were placed around the auditorium to project imagery that had been predistorted, cut, and blended on to this enormous structure. A smaller pop-up screen in the center of the structure was used for moving imagery, as the designers didn't want to make the audience dizzy. The overall complexity and size of the projections hadn't been previously attempted and required specialized software to be developed by Seventh Sense. "This was a space that worked equally well for a car show, business meeting, and a rock concert," says Grant, who used his

previous experience as a designer for the stage to create this impressive dealer event for Ford. "It's all about bringing in theatrical techniques to communicate and create emotional impact," he says.

Lasting three days, the design needed to be adaptable enough to incorporate a 3,000 seat gala dinner, reveals of various new models, the presentation and communication of detailed business information and, finally, a concert by singer Sheryl Crow. The new models were revealed on a slowly spinning revolve that rose from beneath the main stage or at the back of the stage when large "barn doors" on the screen opened. The vehicles were then driven off the stage on concealed ramps, in what Grant terms "car ballets." To create enough floor space (and a hidden "off stage" area for catering, garaging cars, and so on), the entire floor of the arena was lifted by 12 1/2 feet (3.8 meters), which created a 37,000 square foot (11,280 square meter) environment in a space where usually only 20,000 square feet (6,096 square meter) was available.

Lead designers: Martin Grant (3D), Eduardo Braniff (CEO and Creative Director), Candice Brokenshire (integration), Mike Sbotnicki (lighting), Chris Slingsby (projection)
Software design: Seventh Sense
Photos: Courtesy of Imagination

Top: View of stage during the business briefing to dealers.

Top, right: Presentation of new Lincoln models with a drive over the main stage area.

Bottom, right: Overview of arena set for gala dinner.

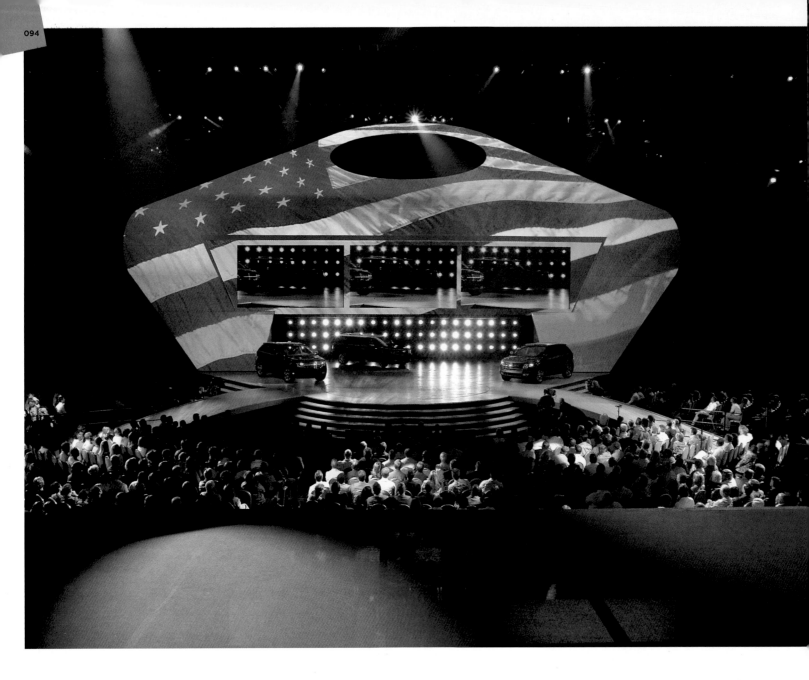

Above: Head-on view of the stage decked out patriotically for the opening of the three-day event.

Top, right: View from the audiovisual control desk.

Bottom, right: Casino-style projections accompanying the presentation of a new Ford model.

New Model Introduction Meeting for Ford Lincoln Mercury

"Ford wanted something completely different that hadn't been done before. This was a dramatic, awe-inspiring shape that also had practical benefits."

Martin Grant, Imagination

"Why not create the first chocolate museum in Mexico and have a 984 foot long façade along the motorway as the new image of the factory?"

Michel Rojkind, Rojkind Arquitectos

Project
Nestlé Chocolate Museum
Design
Rojkind Arquitectos

Above: The museum's auditorium.

Right: The unusual sight greeting visitors to the Nestlé Chocolate Museum.

Client
Nestlé

Location
Mexico City

An extraordinary red structure zigzags out to greet visitors to Nestlé's chocolate factory near Mexico City. Initially, Nestlé simply wanted some sort of access area for visitors wanting to see confectionary being produced, but Michel Rojkind of Rojkind Arquitectos immediately saw potential for something much more involving. "Why not create the first chocolate museum in Mexico and have a 984 foot (300 meter) long façade along the motorway as the new image of the factory?" he asked.

So the client was convinced to implement a more ambitious plan that saw the reception area transformed into a chocolate museum, made up of an impressive welcome area, a store, and an auditorium. The museum ends with a passage to a tunnel inside the factory itself. The entire structure was shoe-horned into a corner of the site.

The playfulness of the building is intentional as school children form a significant part of the target audience, and wowing them was an important consideration. Rojkind also suggests that "alebrijes" (colorful Mexican folk dolls) and origami were influences on the form of the structure. Of course, the striking shape of the museum makes it an attraction in itself, as well as performing an advertising function for Nestlé and its factory to passing traffic.

By getting the extensive project teams to work in shifts, the entire project, from design to finished build, took only two-and-a half months. A steel structure dressed in corrugated panels is carried aloft on top of a concrete base. The interior was painted in different shades of white and gray to further accentuate the "folded" structure.

Structural engineer: Moncad
Landscape design: Ambiente Arquitectos y Asociados
Images: Paúl Rivera/archphoto.com

Top, left: The museum lit up at night, showing how it also functions as a giant billboard. The structure is carried aloft on concrete beams.

Top, center and right: Overviews of the main reception area.

Bottom, right: The entrance to the Nestlé Chocolate Museum.

Above: The staircase up to the main visitor area.

Right: Passageway with atmospheric floor lighting.

Far right: Plan showing the relationship of the new structure to the preexisting factory.

"The striking shape of the museum makes it an attraction in itself, as well as performing an advertising function for Nestlé and its factory to passing traffic."

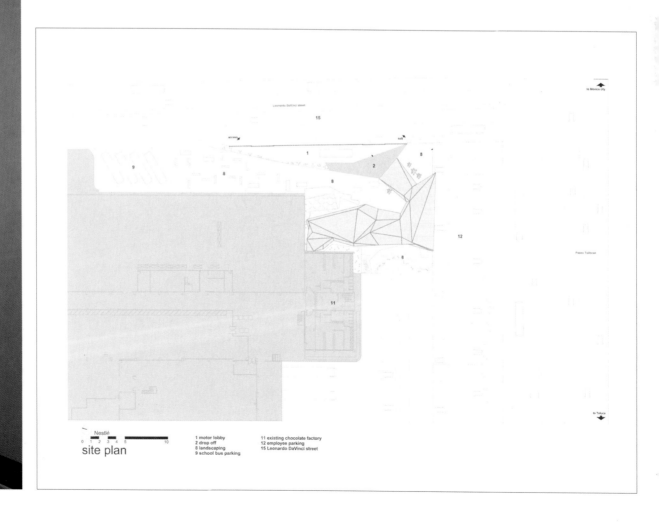

site plan

Nestlé
0 1 2 3 4 5   10

1 motor lobby
2 drop off
8 landscaping
9 school bus parking

11 existing chocolate factory
12 employee parking
15 Leonardo DaVinci street

15 Leonardo DaVinci street

to México city

Paseo Tollocan

to Toluca

DIE
SCHÖNSTEN
FRANZOSEN
KOMMEN AUS
NEW YORK.

FRANZÖSISCHE MEISTERWERK
AUS DEM METROPOLITAN MU
1. JUNI BIS 7. OKTOBER 2007 WW

Project
**Metropolitan Museum of Art,
New York in Berlin**

Design
MetaDesign AG

**Above: Poster outside the Neue
Nationalgalerie for the exhibition
Metropolitan Museum of Art, New
York in Berlin, showing the airmail-
derived branding for the show.**

**Right: One of a selection of posters
for the exhibition.**

Metropolitan Museum of Art, New York in Berlin

Client
Verein der Freunde der Nationalgalerie

Location
Neue Nationalgalerie, Berlin

DIE SCHÖNSTEN FRANZOSEN KOMMEN AUS NEW YORK.

FRANZÖSISCHE MEISTERWERKE DES 19. JAHRHUNDERTS AUS DEM METROPOLITAN MUSEUM OF ART, NEW YORK. 1. JUNI BIS 7. OKTOBER 2007. NEUE NATIONALGALERIE, BERLIN. KULTURFORUM POTSDAMER PLATZ. EINE AUSSTELLUNG DER STAATLICHEN MUSEEN ZU BERLIN. ERMÖGLICHT DURCH DEN VEREIN DER FREUNDE DER NATIONALGALERIE UND DIE WESTLB AG. **WWW.METINBERLIN.ORG**

For a major exhibition to be supported by advertising is nothing new. But a fully integrated campaign approach, drawing on the full array of contemporary branding and marketing techniques, is rarely attempted. But this is just what MetaDesign was able to do, taking its experience of corporate identity and transplanting it to an exhibition of nineteenth-century French paintings loaned from New York's Metropolitan Museum of Art, which was to go on show in Berlin's Neue Nationalgalerie.

The exhibition was expensive to stage and the client wanted to ensure that not only would people be tempted to go to the show, but that a distinctive identity be developed that would also encourage the sale of branded merchandise. "The challenge was to find a powerful idea that would bring the French impressionists to life in people's hearts and minds," says Uli Mayer-Johanssen, MetaDesign's chief design officer, who led the project. She decided to turn the geographic complexity inherent in the show to an advantage. "The creative concept establishes an exciting relationship between the collection's home in America and its origins in France," Mayer-Johanssen explains. "An important component is the color palette, which features the colors of both the American and French flags—red, white, and blue. As a design element, the airmail letter visually represents the paintings' journey across the Atlantic."

Top, left: The "branded" exhibition catalog.

Right: In situ outdoor advertising for the exhibition created by MetaDesign.

Metropolitan Museum of Art, New York in Berlin

"The creative concept establishes an exciting relationship between the collection's home in America and its origins in France. The airmail letter visually represents the paintings' journey across the Atlantic."

Uli Mayer-Johanssen, MetaDesign

This visual identity was then accompanied by the strap line: "Die schönsten Franzosen kommen aus New York" (the most beautiful French people come from New York), which was then widely adopted as the show's informal title. The flexibility and strength of the visual identity was extensively exploited. Not only was there a "branded" catalog, but the show was also supported with advertising around Berlin and in the national press, banners outside the museum itself, and distinctively branded postcards, posters, bags, and other merchandise.

Images: Courtesy of MetaDesign

Top, center; top, right; and bottom, right: Various examples of printed exhibition material.

"The flexibility and strength of the visual identity was extensively exploited. Not only was there a 'branded' catalog, but the show was also supported with advertising around Berlin and in the national press, banners outside the museum itself, and distinctively branded postcards, posters, bags, and other merchandise."

Above: Various examples of magazine advertisements.

Right: A branded bag for the exhibition with merchandise.

Far right: A double-decker bus in Berlin decked out in the exhibition's branding and advertising.

"The official Art Basel
newsletter enthused that
'the container presented
by Kenny Schachter/ROVE
can be regarded as a total
work of art.'"

**Above: Night view of the exterior of
the shipping container converted
into an exhibition space by Zaha
Hadid Architects.**

Z.Box

A series of converted shipping containers at Collins Park Beach, Miami Beach, were the unlikely homes for a variety of exhibitors at the annual Art Basel Miami Beach international art show. While most contained the work of emerging artists, one was designed by Pritzker-winning architect Zaha Hadid.

Commissioned by London-based art impresario Kenny Schachter, it was conceived as a multimedia installation/lounge space to showcase Hadid's recent work. Models and animations of selected projects, including the Aquatic Centre for the London Olympics 2012, the Dubai Dancing Tower, and Singapore Guggenheim, were presented.

The exhibition space was designed as both a further example of the prowess of the Zaha Hadid studio and as an appropriate environment for the presentation of its work. The studio describes the Z.Box as follows: "A swarm of swift geometries choreographs the organization of works on display. Through the interplay of natural and LED light, the reflective interior space evokes a dynamic perceptual experience for visitors. An array of functional elements additionally provide seating and serving within an encapsulated environment."

Left: Interior of the Z.Box, showing the unconventionally dark and disorientating interior.

The resulting space was reminiscent of the black bedrooms that Zaha Hadid designed for the Hotel Puerta America in Madrid. However, polystyrene foam and epoxy polyurethane finishes were used for the Z.Box, and the fabrication process relied on the rapid-prototype technology of CNC milling.

The official Art Basel newsletter enthused that "the container presented by Kenny Schachter/ROVE can be regarded as a total work of art." That may well be an overstatement, and while Hadid is believed to have professed herself unhappy with the results, the Z.Box does nevertheless give a tantalizing glimpse of her practice's abilities in exhibition design.

Design principal: Zaha Hadid with Patrik Schumacher
Project architect: Eddie Can, Chiu-Fai
Lighting design: Isometrix Lighting + Design
Rapid-prototyping fabrication: Idee & Design GMBH
Photos: Simon Hare

Right: External view of a visitor viewing the exhibits inside the Z.Box.

Top, right: Internal close-up showing the interplay between static displays lit behind glass and television screens.

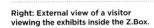

Z.Box

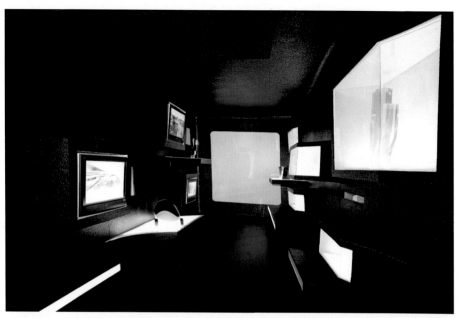

"A swarm of swift geometries choreographs the organization of works on display. Through the interplay of natural and LED light, the reflective interior space evokes a dynamic perceptual experience for visitors."
Zaha Hadid Architects

Left: External view of the Z.Box showing the windows.

Project
Louise T Blouin Institute
Design
Borgos Dance

Client
Louise T Blouin Foundation

Location
London

"The idea was to create a dynamic blank canvas that would allow all different kinds of activities to take place, from installations to fine art, to sound. It's a neutral backdrop, but also a very flexible place."

Simon Dance, Borgos Dance

Far left; top, left; and bottom, left: The exterior of the Louise T Blouin Institute is lit by a permanent installation by James Turrell.

Photos courtesy of the Louise T Blouin Institute. Photography by Richard Davies, 2006.

In a converted industrial building in a neglected corner of west London, the Louise T Blouin Institute takes the concept of the gallery space as "white cube" to its very extreme. The result of a private £20 million ($40 million) investment, the building belies the complexity of its brief to function as a diverse public exhibition space and offices for the Louise T Blouin Foundation.

"The idea was to create a dynamic blank canvas that would allow all different kinds of activities to take place, from installations to fine art to sound," says Simon Dance, who directed the project at Borgos Dance. "It's a neutral backdrop, but also a very flexible place." It is also, he might have added, quite obsessive and flawless, bearing the tell-tale influence of his time working with neo-minimalist architect John Pawson.

The interior of the building was gutted and reengineered to allow for a three-story high reception space and provide the adaptable 5,000 square foot (1,520 square meter) exhibition space behind. A courtyard café was created under glass to the side of the building.

The idea of bringing in artist James Turrell came about during the construction phase and proved serendipitous, with his subtle permanent light installation dovetailing seamlessly with the tightly controlled minimalism of the architecture. All 78 windows and both skylights have invisible, computer-programmed LEDs inserted into them, transforming the building at night. An exhibition of Turrell's work, A Life in Light, served as the institute's inaugural show.

The project is a studied riposte to the move away from the neutral white gallery space. "I am not bothered by fashions, we just wanted to make the best possible exhibition space," says Dance.

Light installation: James Turrell
Lighting design: Campbell Design
Structural engineers: Arup

Top, left: The Courtyard Café created out of a narrow space alongside the building. Photo courtesy of the Louise T Blouin Institute. Photography by Helene Binet, 2006.

Top, right: Reception area of the Louise T Blouin Institute. Photo courtesy of the Louise T Blouin Institute. Photography by Florian Holzherr, 2006.

Right: The 35 foot (10.6 meter) high space of the reception area. Photo courtesy of the Louise T Blouin Institute. Photography by Helene Binet, 2006.

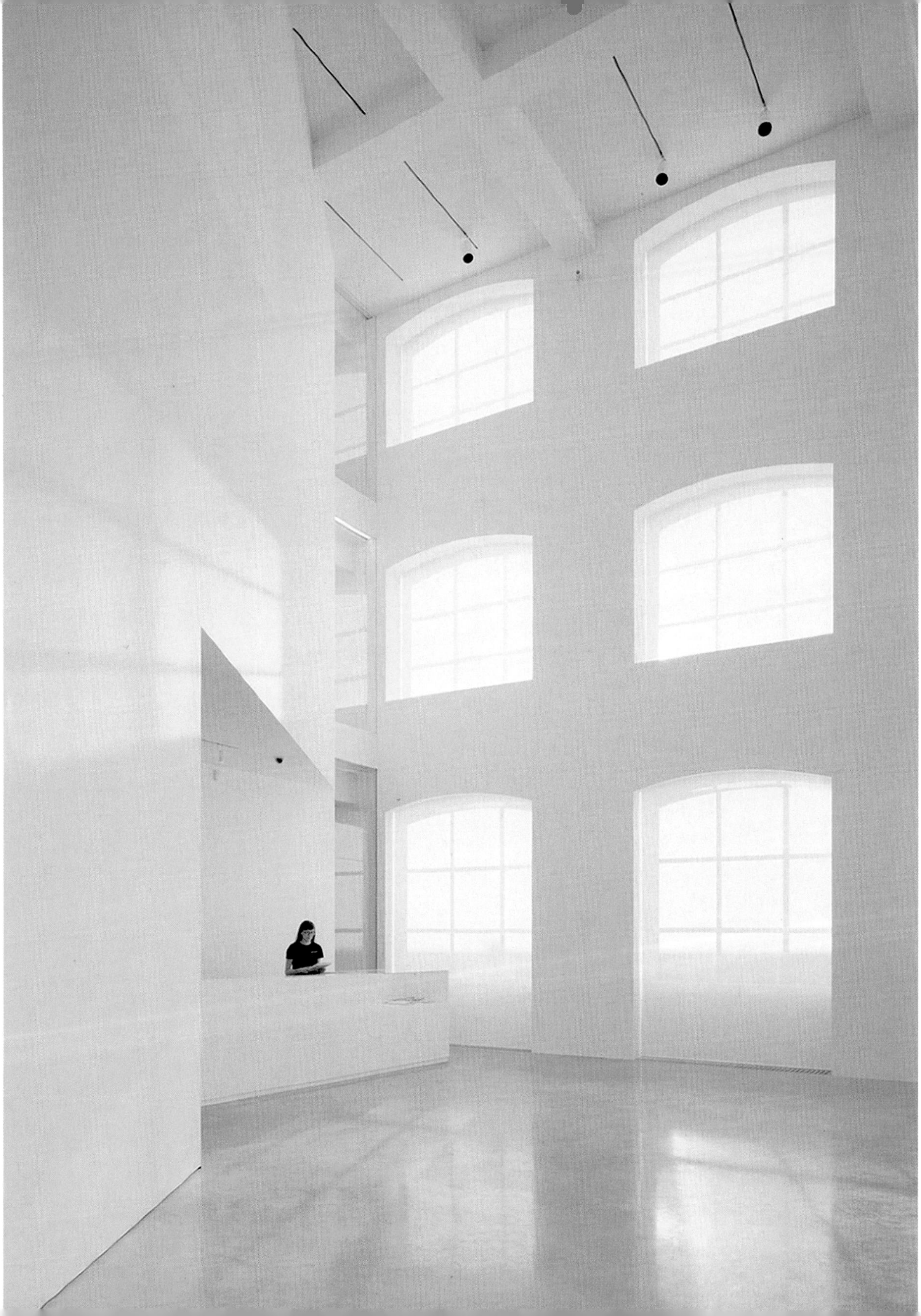

Left and right: The entrance lobby and permanent light installation by James Turrell.

Photos courtesy of the Louise T Blouin Institute. Photography by Richard Davies, 2006.

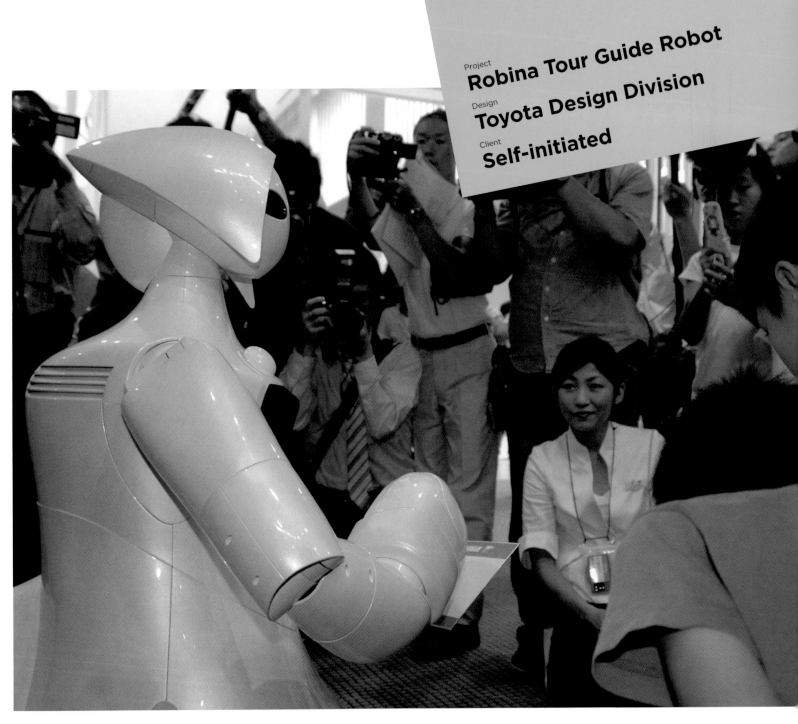

Project **Robina Tour Guide Robot**
Design **Toyota Design Division**
Client **Self-initiated**

Robina Tour Guide Robot

Location

Toyota Kaikan Exhibition Hall, Toyota City

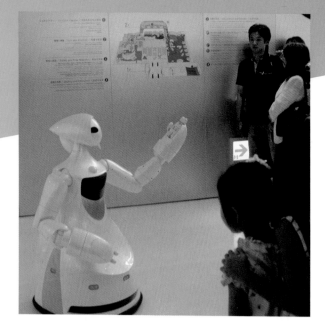

"Taking interactivity to a different level, Robina is able to avoid obstacles, interacts by recognizing and 'speaking' Japanese, and is able to gesture at objects and help visitors."

While technology is viewed with a mixture of fear and awe in many countries, in Japan it is closely bound up with prestige and celebrity. Some robots, such as Mitsubishi's Wakamaru or Honda's Asimo have developed a cult following, but Toyota's contribution to the genre takes its role as an interactive exhibition guide as its starting point.

Robina (an acronym for Robot As Intelligent Assistant) is set on wheels, and can guide visitors around the Toyota Kaikan Exhibition Hall. Taking interactivity to a different level, Robina is able to avoid obstacles, interacts by recognizing and "speaking" Japanese, and is able to gesture at objects and help visitors. Image recognition allows it to recognize visitors from their name tags and its jointed fingers even allow it to sign autographs.

"The robot is able to guide visitors from exhibit to exhibit, in order, and use verbal and nonverbal communication to explain the exhibits to them," says a Toyota spokesman. "It features a name tag image recognition enabling the robot to identify and face visitors, as well as verbal communication technology enabling interaction with them."

Robina has a Japanese vocabulary of about 20,000 words, weighs 132 pounds (60 kilograms), and is 47 1/4 inches (120 centimeters) tall. Technology drawn upon includes laser, ultrasonic, power sensors for the arms, a microphone for speech recognition, image recognition, and wireless LAN. It travels around the exhibition at about 2 1/4 miles per hour (3.6 kilometer per hour).

While its initial role is as an exhibition guide, Toyota is working on developing the technology behind Robina to assist with nursing and medical care, manufacturing, domestic duties, and "short distance personal transport."

Photos: Courtesy of Toyota

Left: Robina signing an autograph at the media opening.

Top, right: Robina greeting and interacting with visitors at the Toyota Kaikan Exhibition Hall.

Project
**Bloch Building, Nelson-Atkins
Museum of Art**
Architecture
Steven Holl Architects

Bloch Building, Nelson-Atkins Museum of Art

Client
Nelson-Atkins Museum of Art

Location
Kansas City

Left: The large water pool, designed together with Walter De Maria, allows for reflections and light effects that join the new and existing buildings.

Top: Detail of the ceiling design which admits natural light.

Above: The five distinct pavilions glow softly at night.

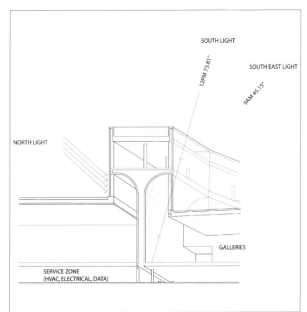

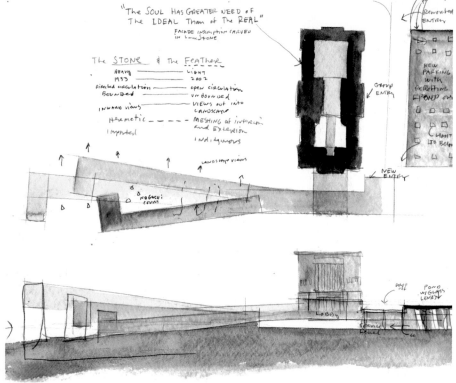

Left: The internal volumes depend on the play of light as much as the exterior of the Bloch Building.

Top, left: Drawing showing the consideration of access of natural light to the galleries.

Above: Watercolor showing how the design of the extension was considered in relation to the existing structures.

Bloch Building, Nelson-Atkins Museum of Art

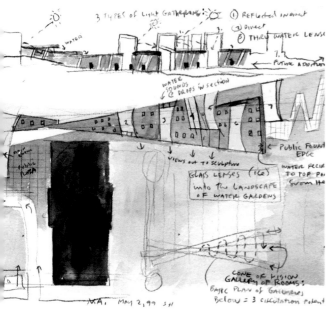

"The 'meandering path' threaded between the lenses in the Sculpture Park has its sinuous complement in the open flow through the continuous level of galleries below. The galleries, organized in sequence to support the progression of the collections, gradually step down into the Park, and are punctuated by views into the landscape."
Steven Holl Architects

Treading with light feet between the bland white cube architecture or the showy self-referentiality of some recent museum building, Steven Holl Architects' extension to the Nelson-Atkins Museum of Art has been widely praised as bringing a new thoughtfulness to the genre without sacrificing any of the experiential theater that is now expected.

The museum needed an extension to house, among other things, its collection of African art, photography, sculpture by Isamu Noguchi, together with a café, ticketing area, and store. Holl's solution was to have a series of five interconnected luminescent structures "meander" down the side of the existing 1930s beaux arts-style museum building, like ice blocks strewn in the park. The blocks, or "lenses," were constructed with multiple layers of glass and computer-controlled filters and layers allow the levels of natural light into the exhibition space to be carefully controlled. During dusk or night, the glowing glass exterior provides what Steven Holl describes as "an inviting transparency, drawing visitors to events and activities." The light structure also allows an easy and natural interplay with the new sculpture park outside and the water installation by minimalist artist Walter De Maria, which captures the reflections of both the existing museum and its new extension.

Notwithstanding its dramatic exterior appearance, it is its ability as a display platform that the museum's management praise. "The building was enriched by Holl's understanding and sense of the museum's collection, and the fact that he drew his design intent from the works of art. Holl saw the building and the collection as partners, always keeping the art in the foreground and using the building as a backdrop," says Barbara Justus at the Nelson-Atkins Museum of Art.

Lighting consultants: Renfro Design Group
Artist: Walter De Maria
Photos: Andy Ryan
Images: Courtesy of Steven Holl Architects

Top, center: The extension at dusk.

Top, right: Architect's watercolor, showing the consideration of different light sources and viewing perspectives.

Bloch Building, Nelson-Atkins Museum of Art

"The building was enriched by Holl's understanding and sense of the museum's collection, and the fact that he drew his design intent from the works of art."

Barbara Justus, Nelson-Atkins Museum of Art

SITE PLAN

1 Entry Plaza
2 Reflecting Pool
3 Lens 1 Lobby
4 Lens 2
5 Lens 3
6 Lens 4
7 Lens 5
8 Original Museum
9 Sculpture Park Lawn
10 Garage Below
11 Garage Entrance

Top, left: The new extension manages to engage harmoniously with the exisiting 1930s classicist museum building.

Bottom, left: Architect's watercolor of the internal space.

Above, center: Detail showing an internal staircase, the polished plaster interior surfaces, and the exterior walls of double-layered glass.

Above, right: Plan of the museum complex.

Project
**Formula One:
The Great Design Race**

Design
Studio Myerscough

Formula One: The Great Design Race

52 51 50

Left: The first display room contained historic cars placed directly on the floor with a timeline down one side of the room.

Above: A Renault F1 car was suspended in "exploded" state over a mirrored base to allow visitors to peer into every nook and cranny.

"It is very important to me that we all understand the whole approach to the project and really understand the subject. It is like being an actor and taking on a role."

Morag Myerscough, Studio Myerscough

Formula One: The Great Design Race

A deceptively simple concept of black gloss flooring, simple yet forthright graphics, and cleverly thought out, non-gimmicky interactives allowed this exhibition devoted to Formula One to speak to a wide audience.

While Formula One has a massive international fan base, this temporary show was intended to appeal to an audience beyond existing aficionados. It was therefore important to draw viewers in to the intricate beauty of the cars. For instance, an exploded Renault F1 car, carefully suspended above a mirrored base, allowed visitors to study in detail an object normally seen only at a distance and at great speed. In a corner, Honda engines with their blocks mounted on castors allowed visitors to touch and engage personally with some very rarified engineering.

By allowing the iconic objects to speak for themselves and permitting close access to normally inaccessible objects, the exhibition proved very successful. Morag Myerscough, who designed the show, attributes this to the close collaboration between herself and independent curator Alicia Pivaro together with Donna Loveday from the Design Museum.

"It is very important to me that we all understand the whole approach to the project and really understand the subject," says Myerscough. "It is like being an actor and taking on a role."

Placing historic cars on the floor rather than on plinths encouraged a psychology of participation, and rare footage screened in the center of the space, featuring some of the legendary figures of the sport, further underscored the romance and excitement of Formula One. The sport has its own characteristic graphic language from checkered flags, pit boards, and the like, and this was co-opted into the design of the show.

Photos: Richard Learoyd

Left: Formula One's characteristic visual identity was incorporated into the show.

Top, left: Various Formula One paraphernalia and car parts, such as tires and exhausts, were made available to touch and inspect, as were some of the engines themselves.

Top, right: A Ferrari F1 car framed by the bold graphics of Studio Myerscough.

"The village structure served as a backdrop, giving the objects a contextual feeling. The layout of the village encouraged open exploration and meandering, without a predetermined path through the show."

Ostap Rudakevych, Studio Lindfors

Project
Design for the Other 90%

Design
Studio Lindfors

Graphic Design
Tsang Seymour Design

Above, left: Tsang Seymour Design's impactful graphics were printed on recyclable cotton.

Above, right: Reclaimed and recyclable materials were used throughout the installation.

Far right: Aerial view of Design for the Other 90%, showing the structure beneath the village-like structure of the outdoor show.

Images courtesy of Design for the Other 90% at Cooper-Hewitt, National Design Museum, Smithsonian Institution. Photographs by Andrew Garn.

Client
Cooper-Hewitt, National Design Museum

Location
New York

In early 2007 something akin to a village was installed in the Arthur Ross Terrace and Garden of the Cooper-Hewitt, National Design Museum in New York. This was an exhibition intended to showcase the ways in which socially responsible design was engaging with the needs of the majority of the world's population. Given the subject matter, the exhibition design by Studio Lindfors and graphic design by Tsang Seymour Design had to have impact while avoiding being incongruous. "Located on Museum Mile, on the busiest avenue in Manhattan, the outdoor location provided a great opportunity to reach the general public," adds curator Cynthia Smith.

"The design strategy was to organize the exhibit into a village-like arrangement with three semicircular walls defining different areas of the exhibition," says Ostap Rudakevych of Manhattan-based Studio Lindfors. "The village structure served as a backdrop, giving the objects a contextual feeling. The layout of the village encouraged open exploration and meandering, without a predetermined path through the show."

Studio Lindfors stressed the use of recycled materials. "One of the greatest challenges we faced when beginning the exhibition design was how to be true to the artifacts and objects that would compose the

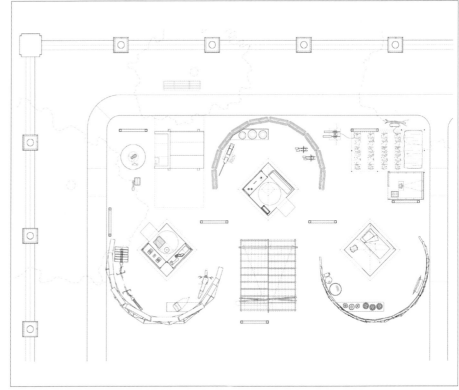

Top: The reclaimed timbers were recycled after the show. Image courtesy of Studio Lindfors.

Bottom, right: Plan showing the layout of Studio Lindfors' design. Image courtesy of Studio Lindfors.

exhibit," says Rudakevych. "Each object seemed to be permeated with a sense of purpose, and innate sense of social responsibility. It is this underlying commonality that compelled us to create an exhibit structure that would support this theme of social responsibility in design.

"To achieve this goal we stressed the use of recycled building components to reduce the amount of usable materials placed in landfills. Informational graphic panels were printed on recyclable cotton canvas rather than typical plastic films. Three curvilinear walls that define and organize the exhibit space were constructed of salvaged materials such as old shipping pallets and heavy timbers pulled from a local warehouse. At the conclusion of the exhibition, a lumberyard purchased the timbers for resale, resulting in zero waste and allowing the exhibit to be just a step in the material's lifecycle."

A website (http://other90.cooperhewitt.org/), designed internally by the museum, allowed the show to have international reach, and featured, among other things, a blog by the curator.

Website: William Berry, Cooper-Hewitt, National Design Museum

Top: More aerial views of the show. Image courtesy of Design for the Other 90% at Cooper-Hewitt, National Design Museum, Smithsonian Institution. Photograph by Andrew Garn.

Above: The introduction to the exhibition. Image courtesy of Studio Lindfors.

Top, left: Simple display of the uses to which bicycles are put. Image courtesy of Studio Lindfors.

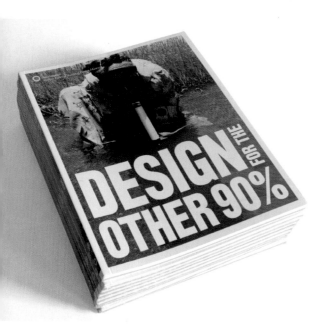

ROLLING WATER

"At the conclusion of the exhibition, a lumberyard purchased the timbers for resale, resulting in zero waste and allowing the exhibit to be just a step in the material's lifecycle."

Ostap Rudakevych, Studio Lindfors

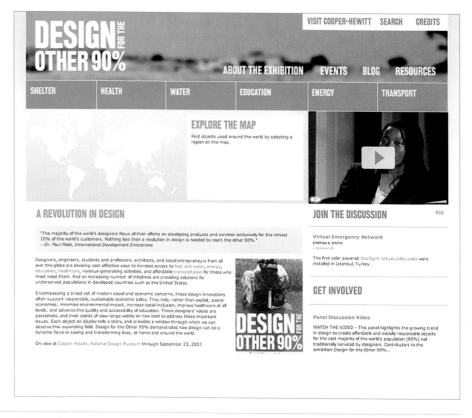

Far left: An aerial view of the show. Image courtesy of Design for the Other 90% at Cooper-Hewitt, National Design Museum, Smithsonian Institution. Photograph by Andrew Garn.

Top, center: Cover of the catalog designed by Tsang Seymour Design.

Top, right: Spread from the accompanying catalog designed by Tsang Seymour Design.

Above: The homepage of the exhibition's website.

"The plinths act as a visual metaphor, elevating these stunning objects into space and beyond their recognized domain. Two raised viewing platforms within the exhibition space mean guests have the opportunity to view these iconic pieces at eye level while those on the ground are forced to navigate and interact with a forest of plinths."

Established & Sons

Project **Elevating Design**

Design **Established & Sons**

Client **Self-initiated**

Above: Visitor level view of the 19 ¹/₂ foot (6 meter) high plinths.

Right: Overview of Elevating Design, showing the provocative plinths and dim lighting.

Elevating Design

To the eerie strains of Gregorian chants being piped loudly around this dimly lit and cavernous space, you could vaguely make out the furniture pieces carved from marble atop plinths some 19 ½ foot (6 meter) high. Reading the brass plaques or captions attached to the enormous and imposing "forest" of plinths only told you what was perched above—to actually see the ostensible exhibit you had a steep climb up to a viewing platform, and even from there the objects were at a haughty and unattainable distance.

This was the British super luxury furniture manufacturers Established & Sons contribution to the 2007 London Design Festival. And if the intention was to deliberately court controversy, the show was a success, proving one of the most talked about events of the festival.

While the works replicated in precious carrara marble were by some of the most stellar names in design today—such as Zaha Hadid, Jasper Morrison, and Amanda Levete—the design of the exhibition itself was the creative brainchild not of a designer, but Established & Sons' CEO (and husband to Stella McCartney) Alasdhair Willis.

"The plinths act as a visual metaphor, elevating these stunning objects into space and beyond their recognized domain," suggested Established & Sons, adding that this was not a selling exhibition.

Reaction was mixed between an appreciation of the theoretical debates about design and art that Established & Sons professed to be presenting, and contemptuous dismissal of the show as the epitome of the pretentiousness and vacuity that has characterized the (lucrative) category of "design art." Willis' own background as a salesman perhaps provides the key to unlocking what is at the heart of the approach.

Images: Courtesy of Established & Sons

Far left: The Aqua Table design by Zaha Hadid for Established & Sons recreated in carrara marble atop a plinth.

Left: The entrance to the exhibition was on the higher level, and accompanied by large-scale graphics. In the foreground is the Drift bench by Amanda Levete, carved out of carrara marble for this show.

Top, center: The Drift-In. Drift-Out, a variation on the Drift bench by Amanda Levete in marble.

Top, right: An adjoining space featured the Drift bench by Amanda Levete, with higher lighting levels to complement the main exhibition.

Project
Herman Miller Showroom
Design
Mauk Design

Client
Herman Miller
Location
NeoCon trade fair, Chicago

"The place was packed with people checking the products out. People had an experience with the products, they weren't just looking at them."
Mitchell Mauk, Mauk Design

For the 2007 NeoCon trade fair in Chicago, office furniture stalwart Herman Miller didn't have any major large furniture launches, but it did have a range of accessories that it needed to present to the world. Most important of these was the Be collection, which includes a desktop climate controller and the Leaf lamp, which has adjustable color temperatures.

"When we were thinking about what to do, we quickly came to the idea that all the senses should be involved," says Mitchell Mauk of San Francisco–based Mauk Design. "So the design was put together to emphasize these things. For instance, for C2 [the mini climate controller], which blows hot and cool, we used thermochromic film to show the temperature changes visually."

Likewise, for the Leaf light, as visitors experimented with its features, changes in its color temperature from warm to cool were lit up typographically behind the products on plexiglass, illuminated from behind by yet another, this time hidden, Leaf light. "The wiring up was a huge challenge," recalls Mauk.

Far left: Overview of the display featuring the diminutive C2 Climate Controller from Herman Miller's Be collection.

Left: Close-up of Leaf display, showing the graphic demonstration of the personal light's color temperature changes. The light was designed by Yves Béhar.

Babble is a small device that scrambles voices to create sound mask, ideal when sensitive or secret discussions are taking place in an open environment. "Again here we wanted a visual cue," says Mauk. "An audiotape played with voices discussing things like divorce or secret plans, but when you pushed the button, the voices scrambled and the lights changed from a red circular pattern to blue and random." The subtle yet didactic exhibits were positioned in glowing white displays with irregular planes, created by backlighting white fabric stretched over a 3 inch (7.6 centimeter) steel frame. "NeoCon is very rigid; there are lots of companies selling modular systems and everything is either vertical or horizontal," explains Mauk. "Our concept was that this would contrast with everything, including the rest of Herman Miller's showroom, to create a dramatic difference. Everything was to be luminescent and glow from within."

The showroom worked both to entice visitors and make them quickly understand the new office accessories. "The place was packed with people checking the products out," says Mauk. "People had an experience with the products, they weren't just looking at them as they were with everything else being presented."

Lead designers: Mitchell Mauk, Larry Raines
Fabrication: Czarnowski

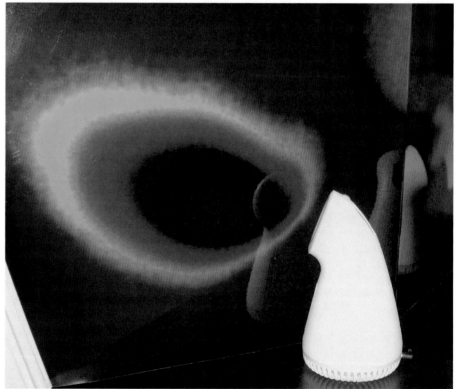

Top, right: Overview of the accessories area of the showroom, showing the structure of stretched fabric over a steel frame.

Above, right: Close-up showing the thermochromic film effects in the C2 display.

Top, far right: For Herman Miller's CMF (Color, Material, Finish) program, Mauk presented the new range in color families, accompanied by a variety of natural and man-made objects, on a shelving structure made of MDF.

"We quickly came to the idea that all the senses should be involved. So the design was put together to emphasize these things. For instance, for C2 [the mini climate controller], which blows hot and cool, we used thermochromic film to show the temperature changes visually."

Mitchell Mauk, Mauk Design

Bottom, left (both images): The Babble display, changing from red circles to a blue random pattern to visually explain the product's voice scrambling function.

Above: The 345 foot (105 meter) long projection screen presenting a journey through the Portuguese language of Brazil.

Far right (both images): The "planetarium of language" that is one of the first experiences greeting the visitor to the museum.

Museu da Língua Portuguesa (Museum of the Portuguese Language)

Client
Fundaçao Roberto Marinho

Location
Saõ Paolo

"The installation speaks to the broadest segment of the population without 'watering down' the content. It is a democratic space."
James Cathcart, Ralph Appelbaum Associates

Above the hustle and bustle of a train station in Saõ Paolo, you will find a museum dedicated to the language that unifies the disparate cultures that make up the vast country of Brazil. Designed by specialist consultancy Ralph Appelbaum Associates, the Museu da Língua Portuguesa (Museum of the Portuguese Language) attempts to create a "sensual and subjective journey through language." With 200,000 people a day using the station accessed beneath, the museum presents itself as a lively, democratic space, filled with the noise of the exhibits and visitors themselves.

The designers decided to retain much of the internal structure of the railway building to impart a feeling of participating in a journey. This is most apparent on the second floor of the museum, the heart of the exhibition, in which a 345 foot (105 meter) long projection screen was installed. Some 36 projectors present 11 different programs dedicated to different aspects of Brazilian culture to which the visitor can walk along. Alongside this is a more traditional presentation, in which relevant artifacts are presented in triangular, internally lit display cases with interactive stations. A separate gallery on the same floor houses the "Etymology Table," a large-scale interactive installation that encourages visitors to play with and discover the etymological roots of the words they use.

Visitors enter the museum from the top; exiting an elevator on the third floor, they are greeted by a screen presentation that then splits to allow them to progress into the Language Plaza, or what the designers call "a planetarium of language." Well-known texts and snippets of music are projected around the room and on to the ceiling, while other texts appear through the glass floor. They descend from there to the main exhibition space, and the lowest floor is shared with the station and its passengers.

"The installation speaks to the broadest segment of the population without 'watering down' the content. It is a democratic space," says James Cathcart, lead designer at Ralph Appelbaum Associates on the project. "It provides an environment where Brazilian culture and language can play themselves out."

Lead designers: James Cathcart, Andres Clerici, Noboru Inoue, Nancy Hoerner
Architects: Paulo and Pedro Mendes da Rocha
Music: Arnaldo Antunes
Photos: Albert Vecerka/Esto, courtesy of Ralph Appelbaum Associates

Top, left: The triangular display boxes and benches adjacent to the main projection screen.

Top, center and bottom, right: Two of the 11 different programs that could be run on the projection screen with its 36 synchronized projectors.

Top, right: The "Etymology Table," an interactive installation allowing visitors to play with the language they use.

"It is a journey through the daily life of Brazil, akin to a train journey. It shows the Portuguese language in daily life, and reveals that language is what holds Brazil together, the technology of all technologies."
James Cathcart, Ralph Appelbaum Associates

Portuguesa (Museum of the Portuguese Language)

Left: Some artifacts were presented in more traditional form.

Above: The main projection screen featuring another of its set programs.

Project:
Hairywood

Design
**6a architects and
Eley Kishimoto**

"The area [around the exhibition] is quite gritty and we thought a tower was the right thing. Hairywood was partly inspired by the top deck of a London double-decker bus; it's slightly voyeuristic."
Stephanie Macdonald, 6a architects

Left: View of Hairywood from across the street, showing how the unusual pattern and textures interact with the adjoining space. Photo by David Grandorge.

Right: The heavily printed canopy that was intended as somewhere for local workers to come and eat their lunch. Photo by David Grandorge.

Client
The Architecture Foundation

Location
The Yard, London

While waiting for its (now cancelled) permanent Zaha Hadid-designed home, The Architecture Foundation wanted to inaugurate its temporary exhibition space, The Yard, with a show about public space. 6a architects partnered with fashion and textile designers Eley Kishimoto to respond playfully to the brief. "We wanted to make a public space rather than create an installation about public space," says 6a's Stephanie Macdonald. "The area [around the exhibition] is quite gritty and we thought a tower was the right thing. Hairywood was partly inspired by the top deck of a London double-decker bus; it's slightly voyeuristic. It was deliberately slightly higher than the bus so you could peer down."

Another inspiration was a scene from Jacques Tati's film, *Les Vacances de Monsieur Hulot*, where the heroine surveys the beach from a small tower of domesticity. "We thought in this case the busy road could function as the beach. We wanted this to be somewhere where people could go and have lunch," adds Macdonald.

"Eley Kishimoto had invited us to work on a project with them before and we asked them to join us on this," says Macdonald. "We worked together from the start, but the roles were very well separated. We didn't

Right: Bench at the top of the tower and the view it afforded. Photo by Tom Emerson.

Top, center: Close-up of a bench, showing the optical play of the heavy patterning by Eley Kishimoto, which was silk-screen printed on industrial printing beds before being frabricated on site. Photo by Tom Emerson.

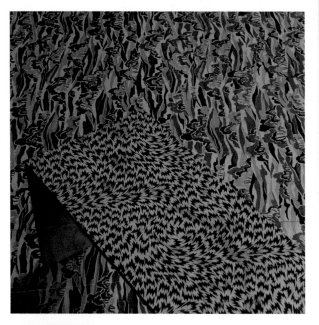

want this to just be a billboard, and it all had to have an associative quality." For instance, the tower's external patterning is compared to "Rapunzel's hair, allowing dappled light into the interior."

The patterns were laser-cut into plywood, which was then weather sealed, and the tower was then constructed out of 2 by 4 inch (5 by 10 centimeter) wood frame. The main internal exhibition space simply had windows covered in laser-cut vinyl and was used primarily for events, such as model building for school children, or entertaining. Hairywood proved so popular that is was kept for double the two-month period initially intended.

Left: Close-up of the laser-cut plywood cladding of the structure. Photo by Tom Emerson.

Top, right: The project at the modeling stage.

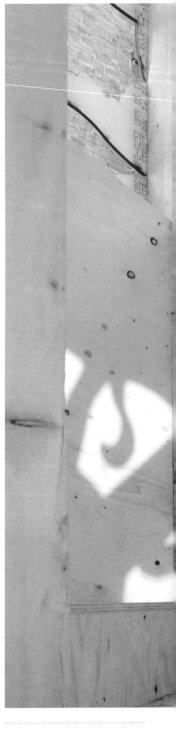

Left: View showing laser-cut vinyl for the main gallery space window. Photo by David Grandorge.

"We wanted to make a public space rather than create an installation about public space."

Stephanie Macdonald, 6a architects

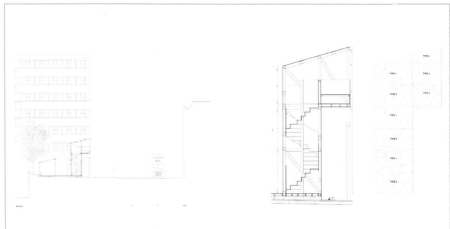

Above, center: Detail showing the staircase inside the tower. Photo by Tom Emerson.

Above, right: Architect's elevation.

Project
The Exchange

Designer/Artist
Peter Freeman

Architecture
MUMA

Above: The glass façade of The
Exchange lit up at night.

Right: Detail from the interior café
area showing the glass ribs and
suffused LED lighting.

Client
Newlyn Art Gallery

Location
Newlyn, Cornwall

"It had to reflect what is in the air and happening around it, whether that is the weather or people walking past. It is a reflective installation, mirroring the way in which the gallery reflects the culture around it."

Peter Freeman

At the western tip of Britain, Cornwall is much loved for the quality of its light and the stunning aquamarines of the sea that surrounds it. While the nearby town of St. Ives is well known for its art galleries, Newlyn's gallery was in need of a revamp. So the museum decided on a two-pronged strategy, overseen by London-based architects MUMA. This saw the existing Victorian seaside building renovated, but, in addition, a nearby former telephone exchange was converted into a gallery, to be known as The Exchange, with the intention that it should function as a landmark for Newlyn.

The director of the museum decided to bring Peter Freeman, a local lighting installation artist, on board at the start of the project. MUMA's addition of a 180 $\frac{1}{2}$ foot (55 meter) long glass wall was conceived as a vehicle for a lighting installation, which Freeman took as a "blank canvas to do something on, a bit like a fresco or mural." His installation relies on barometric and motion sensors, so the lighting interacts and relates to the weather, or senses people walking past and creates a wave of light that seems to follow the person.

"It had to reflect what is in the air and happening around it, whether that is the weather or people walking past. It is a reflective installation, mirroring the way in which the gallery reflects the culture around it,"

Above (both images): Barometric and motion censors vary the display created with LED in three colors: blue, green, and white.

Top, center: The new logo for the two art spaces was created by Cornwall-based graphic design consultancy Absolute Design.

THE
exchange
newlyn
ART GALLERY

explains Freeman. He views the installation as a supplementary work of art, a display that takes place in addition to the exhibitions rather than interacting with them. "When they shut off the lights inside, my work comes into play. It is a nighttime, out-of-hours presence for the gallery."

A series of glass ribs spaced 16 inches (40.6 centimeters) apart are lit by floor-mounted green, blue, and white LEDs that are reflected back to create individual, computer-controlled light tubes.

Graphic design: Absolute Design
Photos: Peter Freeman

Top, right: The installation in an all dark blue phase at night.

Right: Detail showing the color tube created by the glass ribs and metal reflective plates at the top.

OCTOBRE 2005
JANVIER 2006

Project
Dada
Graphic Design
deValence
Client
Centre Pompidou

"The brief for the exhibition graphics was to 'make people understand where they are and what they see in this repetitive, slightly frightening space.'"

Gaël Étienne, deValence

Above: Wall graphic at the Dada exhibition at the Centre Pompidou, designed by deValence. Image © Stéphanie Lacombe.

Right: The catalog was designed not only to synchronize with the exhibition graphics, but also to be an eye-catching presence itself when stacked. Image © Stéphanie Lacombe.

Laurent Le Bon, the curator of the Centre Pompidou's traveling blockbuster exhibition on Dada, wanted the same designers to create the signage and graphics for the show and the accompanying catalog.

So deValence, a graphic design consultancy based in Paris made up of the duo of Alexandre Dimos and Gaël Étienne, was brought on board to work with exhibition designer Jasmin Oezcebi. The enormous exhibition space on the top floor of the Centre Pompidou was subdivided by Oezcebi into a labyrinth of small cells, each dedicated to a particular facet of the Dada movement. The brief for the exhibition graphics, says Étienne, was to "make people understand where they are and what they see in this repetitive, slightly frightening space." And to keep the budget to the very minimum.

deValence's concept for the 1,024-page catalog was to print it on very cheap, low-quality paper, and this approach was transferred to the exhibition graphics. "We used very cheap technologies such as laser (and occasionally ink-jet) prints on uncoated paper, pasted on card, and then pasted on the wall," recalls Étienne. "Our aim was to avoid any interference with the works that were shown. We wanted to accompany this project with discreet but tough design and avoid any imitation of so-called 'Dada design.'"

Not only was the concept shared, but so were the actual fonts used. "This is Dada Grotesk, that we redesigned using specimens we found in some Dada footage from 1917 to 1918. This font is full of errors, but we like it because of it. The italic version was just slanted, with no optical corrections," says Étienne. deValence has since developed this into a commercially available font for Swiss type foundry Optimo.

Exhibition design: Jasmin Oezcebi
Images: Courtesy of deValence

Top, left: Detail of the wall graphics, which deliberately avoided seeming either too slick or too Dada. Image © Stéphanie Lacombe.

Top, center: Front and back cover of the Dada catalog designed by deValence.

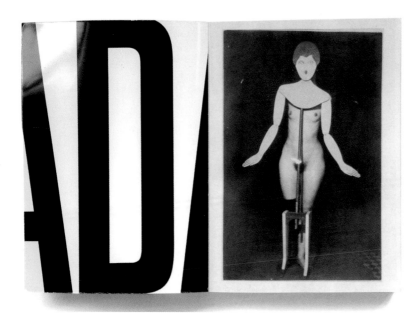

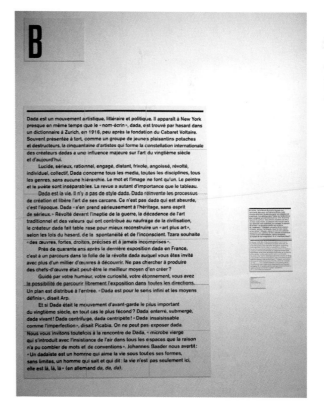

Top and above, center: Opening spread, and further spread, of the catalog.

Above, right: The information graphics were deliberately kept simple, and were just laser-printed, mounted on card, and pasted on the walls. Image © Stéphanie Lacombe.

"Our aim was to avoid any interference with the works that were shown. We wanted to accompany this project with discreet but tough design and avoid any imitation of so-called 'Dada design.'"

Gaël Étienne, deValence

Above, left; above, right; and far right: deValence's signage was designed to help visitors orient themselves in the labyrinthine layout of the show.

> "The Loisium is a mix between museum and modern architecture, historic wine cellars and current cellar technologies, storytelling machine and shopping opportunities."
>
> **Steiner Sarnen Schweiz**

Project
Loisium Visitor Center

Exhibition Design
Steiner Sarnen Schweiz

Architecture
Steven Holl Architects

Loisium Visitor Center

Client
Loisium Hotelbetriebs

Location
Langenlois

Left: The Loisium Visitor Center is an unexpected sight in the middle of the vineyards whose wine it promotes. Image courtesy of LOISIUM/ Robert Herbst.

Above: Installation demonstrating the transformation of fruit juice into wine at the start of the underground visitor tour. Image courtesy of LOISIUM/Robert Herbst.

Loisium Visitor Center

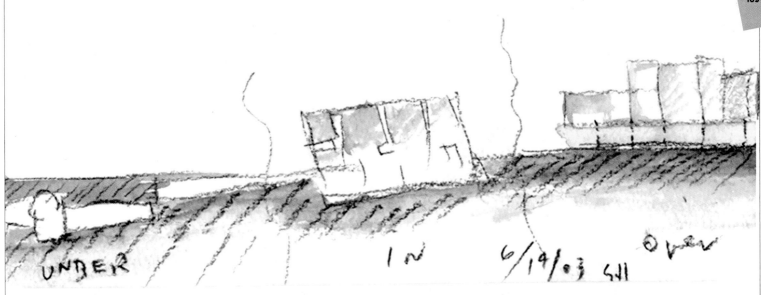

An impressive subterranean maze of 900-year-old tunnels, used for storing wine, were to house a visitor reception area to promote the wines of Lower Austria. But following discussions with Swiss exhibition designers, Steiner Sarnen Schweiz, the idea was hatched of creating something considerably more ambitious. A chance meeting between the Loisium managing director's Finnish wife and Steven Holl, and a discussion about his Kiasma Museum of Contemporary Art in Helsinki, led to the US architect being commissioned to create a structure that would act as a focal point for the vineyards and transport the experience to another level. The result is, in the words of Steiner Sarnen Schweiz, "a mix between museum and modern architecture, historic wine cellars and current cellar technologies, storytelling machine and shopping opportunities."

The visitor experience starts underground in the vaulted wine cellar. The "Gaerdom," a water game that shows how fruit juice is transformed into wine, is followed by a display of the traditional wine-making methods of the historic winery of Anton Loiskandl and the present modern facility. The subterranean tour concludes with a mystical Dionysian installation that, with the merest hint of irony, honors the wine god Bacchus.

After this tour of the historic wine cellars, the visitor emerges into a striking aluminum-clad structure (inspired by wine bottle coverings) that is slightly tilted down the slope under which the subterranean tour takes place. Recycled wine bottles were used for some of the green-hued glazing, and the space, with its roof terrace, functions as a wine store, café, and seminar space.

Winning plaudits from around the world, the Loisium has been successful in attracting attention to Austria's vineyards, and a couple of years after opening, an 82-room luxury hotel, also designed by Steven Holl Architects, was built alongside the visitor attraction.

Far left: The wine altar. Image courtesy of LOISIUM/Robert Herbst.

Top, left: Interior of the Loisium, showing the use of materials that evoke wine making, including green glass produced from recycled wine bottles. Image courtesy of LOISIUM/Robert Herbst.

Bottom, left: A bottle of the local wine with a watercolor by Stephen Holl adapted as a label.

Top, right: Watercolor by Stephen Holl, showing the relationship of the three elements (underground cellars, visitor reception area, and hotel) to the site, demonstrating also the angle to which the Loisium is tilted.

Watercolor courtesy of Stephen Holl Architects.

Loisium Visitor Center

Left: Tasting area in the vinotheque. Image courtesy of LOISIUM/ Robert Herbst.

Top: The 900-year-old vaulted cellar had "prayer wheels" with Dionysian imagery installed as part of the experience. Image courtesy of LOISIUM/Robert Herbst.

Above: Light playing on the aluminum exterior of the Loisium at sunset. Image courtesy of LOISIUM/ Robert Herbst.

Project
365: AIGA Annual Design Exhibition 27

Design
Design360, Inc.

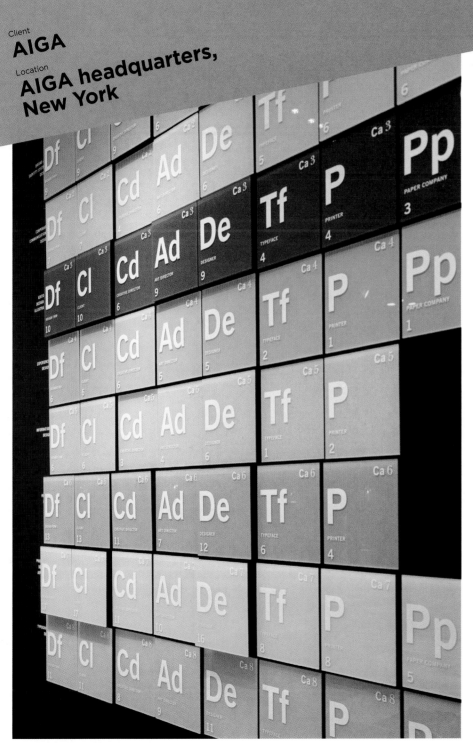

Client
AIGA

Location
AIGA headquarters, New York

"Our inspiration became a scientific laboratory: a blackboard wall to leave comments on and a periodic table of elements."

Jill Ayers, Design360, Inc.

Far left: Overview of the exhibition, showing the giant wall-mounted periodic table.

Left: The oversize periodic table was constructed from back-painted vinyl squares.

When invited by the AIGA to collaborate on its annual design exhibition at its national headquarters in New York, Design360 came up with the idea of transforming the space into what would, in effect, be a creative laboratory.

"The concept was inspired by the creative process," says Design360's Jill Ayers. "As designers, we asked ourselves, what elements—people, processes, materials, and so on—did it take to create these pieces and how can we best illustrate that through a fun exhibit design."

The show was built around the winning entries to AIGA's competition for the year's best communication design. "The elements we created were not designed to distract from the viewers' experience, but inform it," explains Ayers. "Our inspiration became a scientific laboratory: a blackboard wall to leave comments on, a periodic table of elements, labware filled with various creative materials and lab tables. Visitors could walk in and experience the work laid out on each table, organized by category, or interact with the exhibit by leaving comments on the blackboard wall which transformed the space over the duration of the exhibition."

Top, right: Detail showing the colored line graphic that continues from wall to floor to give identity to separate parts of the show.

Right: General view showing exhibit tables and the interactive wall painted with blackboard paint sourced from Benjamin Moore Paints.

"Visitors could walk in and experience the work laid out on each table, organized by category, or interact with the exhibit by leaving comments on the blackboard wall which transformed the space over the duration of the exhibition."

Jill Ayers, Design360, Inc.

The oversized periodic table was a device for linking up the people and processes making up each competition entry. In it, a design firm became "DF," client "Ci," a paper company "Pc," and the binding method "Bm." The idea was that this would enable the viewer to experience relationships and contrasts between category and content.

Color coding was carried through from the periodic table to the displays and design-related labware contents. The visitor was helped by lines on the floor which defined which table and wall-mounted exhibits belonged in the same category.

The project was executed to a tight budget, and environmental considerations were taken into account. "To conserve resources, we retrofitted the AIGA's existing work tables to simulate the lab environment, therefore creating less waste," says Ayers. "The flexible tabletop signage will be flipped over and used again for future exhibits."

Lead designers: Jill Ayers, Rachel Einsidler
Photos: Jennifer Krough

Above: View of the exhibition from the street.

Project
Gameworld

Design
Leeser Architecture

Client
**Laboral Centro de Arte
y Creación Industrial**

Location
Gijón

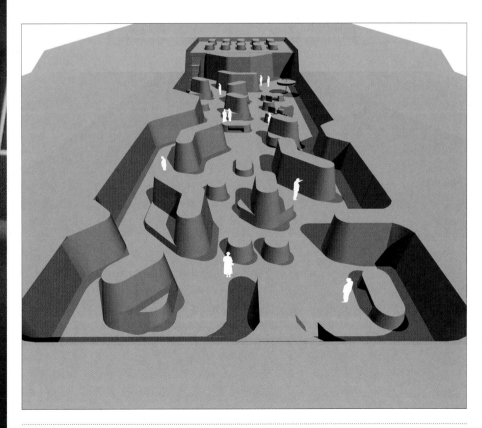

**Left: The "unreal" blue landscape
of Gameworld.**

**Above: Virtual presentation of the
exhibition space that visitors could
navigate on a large screen on
entering the exhibition.**

> "This unreal landscape is entirely executed in digital blue amplifying the physical tactility while at the same time producing an effect of slightly absurd mono-materiality."
>
> **Leeser Architecture**

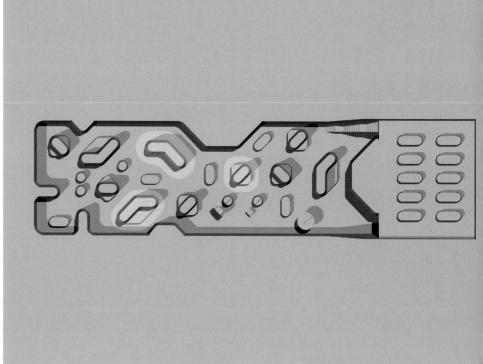

Bottom, left: Different colors marked out different "levels" that had been achieved, as in a computer game.

Above: Bird's eye virtual view of the exhibition layout.

One of the opening exhibitions of this ambitious space, attached to the University of Laboral, Gijón, in the Asturias region of Spain, was dedicated to the computer game. Designed by New York architecture practice Leeser, and entitled Gameworld, it constructed a deliberately confusing landscape, blurring the distinctions between the real and the simulated world of the computer game or digital art.

The installation consisted mainly of mounds that assumed different shapes and functions according to the part they had to play. Deliberately slightly taller than the visitors, the restricted sight lines served to heighten a perception of being immersed in an unreal terrain of valleys and mountains.

"Navigation within this landscape becomes the primary objective of this world," explain the designers. "Not only the navigation from module to module, but also deep within each module as the exhibition visitor explores the many worlds of the gaming experiences featured."

Emulating video games, the exhibition was conceived as a series of temporal levels, with color used as articulation: "Blue is the color of this world's first level. As the exhibit advances to level 2, level 3, or beyond, the blue modules are replaced by those with new games and installations and subsequently made of a different color. The modules become pink in level 2, until eventually the entire environment has been reclaimed and recolored."

Giant screens at the entrance presented the exhibition space virtually, so the visitor had the vertiginous option of navigating the space both in the digital and actual realm and directing one from the other.

Images: Courtesy of Leeser Architecture

Top, left: Overview of the actual exhibition, showing the varied uses to which the pods were put.

Top: Close-up of the pods, showing their overbearing height in comparison to a visitor.

"Navigation within this landscape becomes the primary objective of this world, not only the navigation from module to module, but also deep within each module as the exhibition visitor explores the many worlds of the gaming experiences featured."

Leeser Architecture

Above: The pods were covered in felt.

Right: Dramatic lighting accentuated the unreal nature of the environment created for the show.

Project
Visual Identity for Mori Arts Center
Design
Barnbrook Design
Lead Designer
Jonathan Barnbrook

Client
Mori Arts Center

Location
Tokyo

"All the waveforms, when combined, make up the logo of the Mori Arts Center. The spectrum and waveforms represent an organization made up of many disparate parts, which, as a whole represent the whole gamut of the arts and society which work together."

Jonathan Barnbrook

Far left: Poster for the inaugural Happiness show at the Mori Arts Center, designed by Barnbrook Design and featuring the bespoke font used for all the center's communications.

Left: Poster designed by Barnbrook Design for the Happiness exhibition.

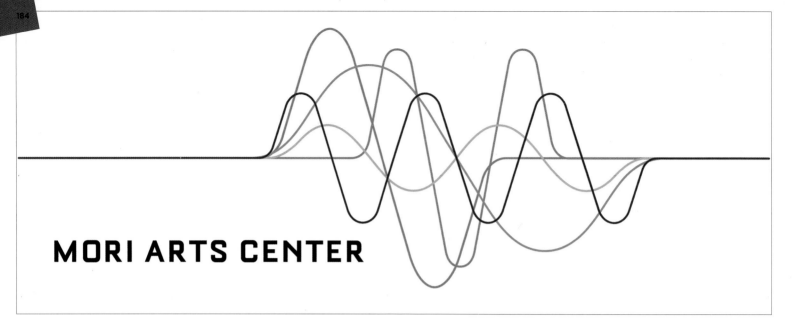

MORI ARTS CENTER

Modern cultural institutions are now many layered organizations. The core cultural attraction often exists in association with rival attractions, stores, restaurants, schools, and beyond. So when British graphic designer Jonathan Barnbrook created the logo for Tokyo's Mori Arts Center, perched at the top of the 54-story Roppongi Hills Mori Tower, he made this multifaceted approach a feature of the visual identity, literally combining the various strands.

In this case, apart from the contemporary art gallery, there was an observation gallery (Tokyo City View), the stores and restaurants that make up the Roppongi Hills Club, a school (Roppongi Hills Academy), and the Tokyo Sky Deck roof gardens to consider. As well as providing both an overarching umbrella identity, each part had to have its own identity and work in both Japanese and English.

"We were asked to come up with a logo that reflected what the Arts Center was about, but was also made up of all of the logos of the subsections," explains Barnbrook. "The solution was to use the idea of 'spectrum.' Each subsection was assigned a different color from the light spectrum and a particular waveform for its own corporate identity. All the waveforms, when combined, make up the logo of the Mori Arts Center. All the waveforms work as independent logos. The spectrum and waveforms represent an organization made up of many disparate parts which as a whole represent the whole gamut of the arts and society which work together."

As well as the identities (which use the bespoke font Mori), Barnbrook Design oversees most of the visual content issued by the organization, from its website to catalogs and merchandise.

Images: Courtesy of Barnbrook Design

Top: The main identity for the Mori Arts Center, which incorporates the different wavelength identities of the subsidiary attractions, and which is presented in animated form on its website.

A B C D E F G H I J K L
M O R I A R T S C E N T E R
S T U V X Y W Z

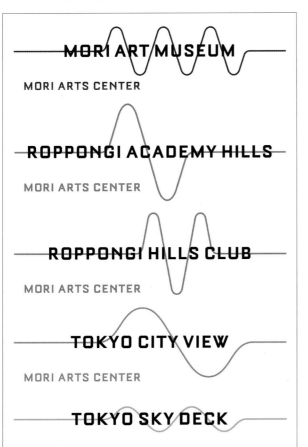

Left: The five subsidiary identities, when superimposed, form the main Mori Arts Center identity shown top left.

"The solution was to use the idea of 'spectrum.' Each subsection was assigned a different color from the light spectrum and a particular waveform for its own corporate identity."

Jonathan Barnbrook

Top: The "clean and modern" bespoke font created by Barnbrook Design for the Mori Arts Center.

Above, left; above, center; top, left; and far right: Barnbrook Design was also responsible for designing merchandise for the center, as well as all its communication materials.

Visual Identity for Mori Arts Center

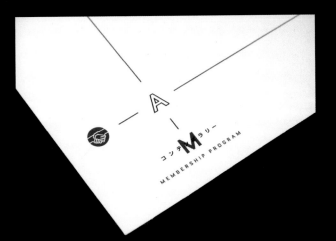

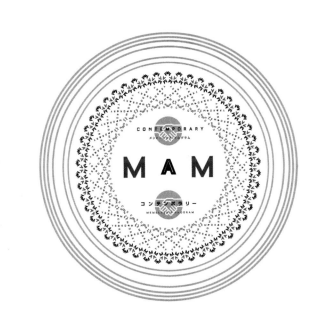

> "The room is a large piece of furniture that you are invited to explore. The brief was not to overwhelm visitors, but invite them to explore further."
>
> **Gitta Gschwendtner**

When the Wellcome Trust, a large and powerful medical charity, chose to have a public face in the center of London, it decided to commission two permanent exhibitions alongside the usual café, public library, and temporary exhibition space. One was to be dedicated to the collection of medical curiosities amassed by its founder, Sir Henry Wellcome, while the other was to showcase the start of art in contemporary medicine.

For the first of these exhibitions, entitled Medicine Man, Gitta Gschwendtner decided to solve the problem of having two separate entrances with what she terms a "Wunderkammer," a large central display that captures the eccentricity of Sir Henry Wellcome as well as providing a useful vehicle for the medical and anthropological artifacts he collected.

"I wanted to evoke the general mood of a dark and moody Victorian study with walnut and dark finishes, which, as they acquire patina, will only add to the effect," says Gschwendtner.

Far left: Central Wunderkammer display fixture greeting the visitor entering Medicine Man from either of the two entrances. Photos on these pages by Sorted.

Top, left: Overview of Medicine Now, showing the tilted red cubes that house interactive installations. **Bottom, left:** Entrance to Medicine Now, showing the three-dimensional graphics designed by Kerr|Noble.

To encourage a sense of discovery, Gschwendtner designed the room as "a large piece of furniture that you are invited to explore." She adds, "The brief was not to overwhelm visitors, but invite them to explore further if they want." To entice the viewer in, some of the exhibits and captions are hidden away in drawers or behind panel doors.

In contrast, the adjoining exhibition, Medicine Now, is modern and light. By specifying Corian for the furniture, Gschwendtner was able to use bright white furniture for a permanent exhibition without worrying about it dirtying. Red cubes, which contain either interactive displays or contemporary art with medical themes, were constructed out of powder-coated steel, to ensure they are equally durable. But the exhibition furniture also had a subliminal function. "Devices such as the very tall shelving imply there is much more information than can be shown," says Gschwendtner, whose initial training was as a furniture designer.

Unusually, Gschwendtner and graphic designers Kerr|Noble worked together on the project right from the start. "Graphics are often an afterthought. This was a lot more difficult and interesting; with an integrated approach like this, the graphics can influence the

three-dimensional space and vice versa," explains Frith Kerr. "We didn't want to just drop a captions system into Gitta's minimalist design."

Instead the design evolved so that the exhibition furniture has grooves containing the captions, and some of the lettering (set in Houschka) became a sculptural and totally integrated part of the design.

A further element of collaboration is apparent in the feedback wall, in which hand-drawn notes from visitors are pasted on the back wall to form part of the display that contrasts vividly with the modernity of the rest of the room.

Graphics: Kerr|Noble
Interactive content: ico Design Consultancy

Top, left: Cabinet with drawers containing further exhibits at one end of Medicine Man. Photo by Sorted.

Top, center: Captions were also hidden behind doors. Photo by Sorted.

Top, right: The feedback wall at the back of Medicine Now, with a table for visitors to sit and write their thoughts. Photo by Sorted.

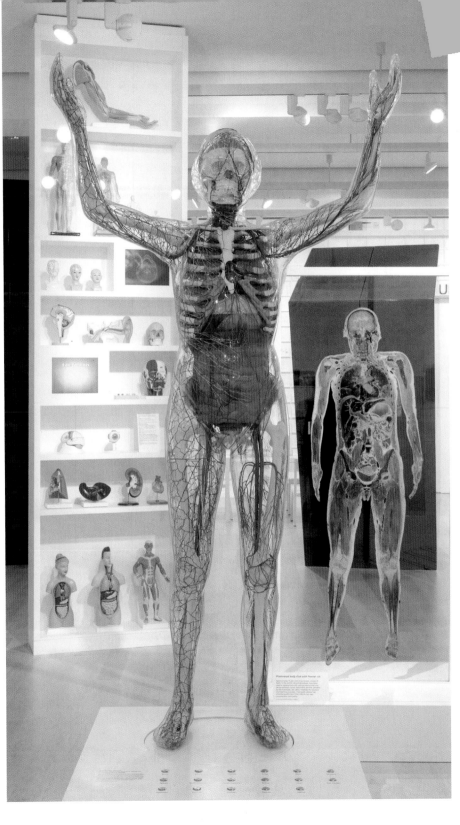

Above, left: Detail showing the kind of feedback posted on the wall. Photo by Sorted.

Right: The dramatic central exhibit of Medicine Now, with oversize furniture in the background. Photo by Sorted.

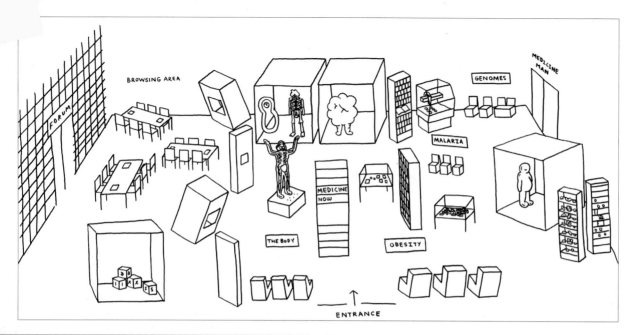

Top, left: "The client wanted an architectural map, but we thought that wouldn't be too helpful, so we commissioned illustrator James Graham to do a drawing instead," explains Frith Kerr.

Bottom, left: Detail of central Wunderkammer, showing the atmospheric lighting. Photo © Wellcome Library, London.

Bottom, right: Overview of Medicine Now, showing the listening chairs (which play information to people sitting on them) and the first ever complete print out of the human genome in bound volumes on the bookshelf behind. Photo © Wellcome Library, London.

Opposite, top: One of several interactives designed by ico Design Consultancy, in which the faces of successive visitors are blended with previous participants to give an "average" face.

Opposite, bottom: The back of the central Wunderkammer is covered with paintings from the Wellcome collection with a medical theme. Photo © Wellcome Library, London.

Medicine Man and Medicine Now

Project
Museum of Broken Relationships

Design
Drazen Grubisic and Olinka Vistica

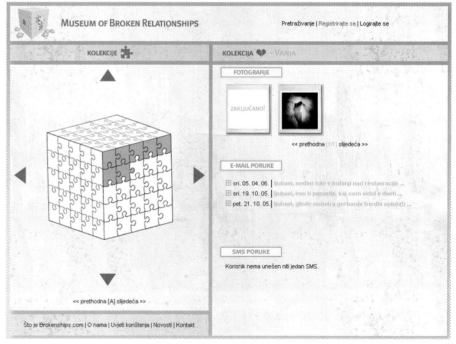

Far left: This converted shipping container in Zagreb, Croatia, is one of the repositories of the Museum of Broken Relationships.

Bottom, left: A teapot that was donated as a memento of a defunct relationship.

Top, right: The homepage of the website: www.brokenships.com.
Above, right: Inside the virtual museum online.

"It is very democratic, if you donate something with a short description, we will put it in a museum. It is anonymous, and if it doesn't offend anyone, it will be displayed. So we may say that we have succeeded in having real interactivity."

Drazen Grubisic

Museum of Broken Relationships

Turning interactivity on its head, the Museum of Broken Relationships asks its visitors to supply the exhibits. Bring an object that testifies to a relationship that is now over, along with a description, and it will become a part of this cathartic "museum" conceived by Drazen Grubisic and Olinka Vistica after their own breakup.

The Museum of Broken Relationships exists online (at www.brokenships.com) or as part of a modular traveling show. It's an art project that masquerades as an exhibition, using the stock in trade of display as an emotional tool. Shows in Croatia and Slovenia, and then at the Tacheles gallery in Berlin, received a surprising amount of media attention; its unique form of interactivity touching a chord with an enthusiastic public, leading to more staging posts, or collection points, being organized.

"The objects have to be seen together with their descriptions," says Grubisic. "Some not so spectacular objects are pretty emotional when you read the description. An axe, a pen, a gallstone, an artificial leg, a bicycle, a cellphone, a wristwatch, to name but a few."

"It is very democratic, if you donate something with a short description, we will put it in a museum. It is

anonymous, and if it doesn't offend anyone, it will be displayed. So we may say that we have succeeded in having real interactivity," he adds.

The idea behind the Museum of Broken Relationships is that objects contain memories and emotions almost as integrated fields or holograms, and that the display provides "a space of 'secure memory' or 'protected remembrance.'" Grubisic and Vistica contrast this to the superficial world of television and online advice: "Unlike the 'destructive' self-help instructions for recovery from broken relationships, the Museum offers every individual the chance to overcome the emotional collapse through creation, by contributing to the holdings of the Museum."

Photography: Ana Opalic

Bottom, left: The actual modular display furniture was kept very simple allowing it to travel easily.

Top, left: A wedding dress that testifies to a broken relationship, with accompanying materials and text provided by the donor to explain the sorry tale.

Top, center: A donated glass horse statuette with its accompanying story.

Top, right: Two stuffed toys that told a tale.

"I created a dream garden of lightness, a garden of wonders. A place in which to experience life at a different pace, of life connected to the uncertainty of new alliances, dance connected to space and sound."

Marcel Wanders

Project
Marcel Wanders Personal Editions

Design
Marcel Wanders

The large, reclaimed industrial space of Ex Ansaldo, in the fashionable Via Tortona area of Milan, was chosen by superstar designer Marcel Wanders for an exhibition of his own limited-edition furniture at the 2007 Salone del Mobile (Milan Furniture Fair).

One of design's more controversial figures, the presentation of himself as an auteur and brand, was reminiscent of the world of fashion. Presented under the rubric Personal Editions, the furniture and accessories were clearly not mass-produced, relying instead on handmade craft and rapid prototyping techniques. The environment these bespoke objects were presented in had to overwhelm the visitor with the possibilities his antimodernist design philosophy opens up. Scale and pattern both violate traditional design norms, but transformed the space into an Alice in Wonderland-like environment, in the process creating blue water between itself and the conventional trade show stand.

"Design can outgrow its traditional cultural value and aspire to work on a grander scale, giving more, moving the hearts of its audience in unknown, deeper, and more individual directions," says Wanders. These were sentiments that were interpreted quite literally for this installation.

Right: The heavily patterned floor draws attention down from the industrial ceiling and creates an otherworldly environment for the bespoke creations of Marcel Wanders.

Far right: As designer of the environment and objects on display, Wanders was able to make the most of the games of scale intrinsic to the furniture. Both photos by Inga Powilleit, styling by Tatyana Quax.

Marcel Wanders Personal Editions

Client
Self-initiated

Location
**Salone del Mobile,
Ex Ansaldo, Milan**

Above: The show remained a selling trade show exhibition, as testified by a brand-reinforcing image of Wanders himself on the wall. Photograph courtesy of Marcel Wanders Studio.

Top, center: The design plays witty and complicated games with traditional aesthetics. Photograph courtesy of Marcel Wanders Studio.

Bottom, right: Though not mentioned by Wanders, Alice in Wonderland was a clear reference. Photograph by Nicole Marnati.

"Design can outgrow its traditional cultural value and aspire to work on a grander scale, giving more, moving the hearts of its audience in unknown, deeper, and more individual directions."

Marcel Wanders

"I wanted to go beyond the sentiments and needs of daily life to create a sense of wonder. Design is a tool that allows us to reach out and inspire, to touch others, and help make lives magic and wonderful," continues Wanders. "I created a dream garden of lightness, a garden of wonders. A place in which to experience life at a different pace, of life connected to the uncertainty of new alliances, dance connected to space and sound. Frozen flower fossils spring to life. Topiary and flowers meld, forming carefully sculpted characters."

Top, right: View of the installation that most closely aligns it with traditional furniture stands. Photograph by Inga Powilleit, styling by Tatyana Quax.

Project
**Literaturmuseum der Moderne
(Museum of Modern Literature)**
Design
David Chipperfield Architects

Literaturmuseum der Moderne (Museum of Modern Literature)

Client
Deutsches Literaturarchiv Marbach

Location
Marbach am Neckar

"The architectural language of the museum building with its almost archaic piles of horizontal and vertical sticks tries not to comment on language and literature, but simply on architecture itself."

Alexander Schwarz, David Chipperfield Architects

Left: The beautifully restrained exterior of the Literaturmuseum der Moderne.

Left: Interior showing the interplay between the dark wood-paneled walls, giant doors, the concrete structure, limestone floors, and glass displays.

Top: Display cabinets for the manuscripts and books in the artificially lit exhibition galleries.

Literaturmuseum der Moderne (Museum of Modern Literature)

A visitor climbs to the top of a rocky plateau to see the austere colonnade of the terrace of the Literaturmuseum der Moderne (the Museum of Modern Literature), situated to the side of an existing fin de siècle museum building, and looking out across the valley like a Greek temple.

This pavilion-like volume, located on the highest terrace, provides the entrance to the museum. As the visitor descends downstairs and through massive doors, the various parts of the museum interior reveal themselves, until they reach the exhibition galleries. These dark paneled rooms house a flickering display of glass cabinets. While these are illuminated solely by low-level artificial light in deference to the sensitivity of the works on display, each gallery has an adjacent open space with views across the valley, representing spatially the interiority of the practice of reading literature and its relation to the external world.

"Due to its location next to the Schiller Nationalmuseum, the Museum of Modern Literature has a cultural as well as a panoramic dimension," explains Alexander Schwarz, the lead architect for the project at David Chipperfield Architects, Berlin. "However the exhibits themselves—mainly sheets of paper with ink on them—required rooms which create intimacy and a visual

calm and, due to their fragility, darkness and low temperatures. The architecture attempts to enjoy both qualities—the daylight together with the views from the concrete terraces over the valley and the darkness of the timber-clad, artificially lit exhibition spaces in the base below the terraces. The sequence of the space creating the transition between these two qualities is crucial for the experience of the museum."

The neoclassical structure has more than a nod in the direction of grand museum architecture of the past. Or as Schwarz puts it, "the architectural language of the museum building, with its almost archaic piles of horizontal and vertical sticks, tries not to comment on language and literature, but simply on architecture itself."

The project won the 2007 RIBA Stirling Prize, the UK's highest architectural accolade.

Cabinet maker/interior fitting: Friedrich Hanselmann KG Möbel und Innenausbau
Photos: Christian Richters
Plans: Courtesy of David Chipperfield Architects

Top: Installation of poetry by Hans Magnus Enzensberger.

Literaturmuseum der Moderne (Museum of Modern Literature)

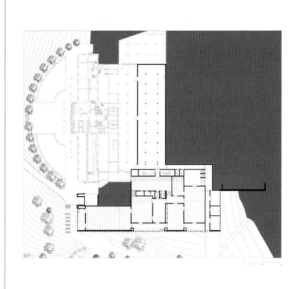

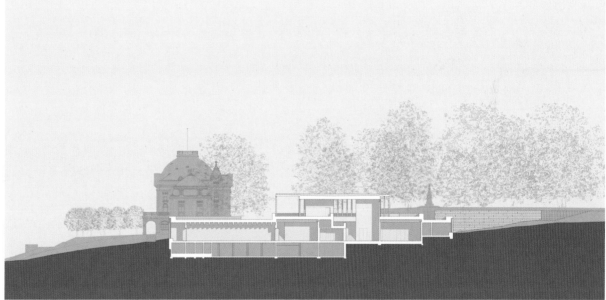

Left: Interior of the entrance pavilion to the museum.

Top: Plan showing the relationship of the Literaturmuseum der Moderne to the adjacent Schiller Nationalmuseum.

Above: Elevation showing the subterranean design of the museum.

A POSTMAN'S DIARY

WHERE ARE YOU? (05)

Text and Drawings: Kevin Boniface
Photographs: Shaw&Shaw

P534CT   RAS0380001

On the landing I told Ian about the Dead Pigeon Man and he told me about his mates Grandad who was so poor that he used to go out on a Friday night and collect bits of meat from pools of sick in the street and fry them up when he got home.

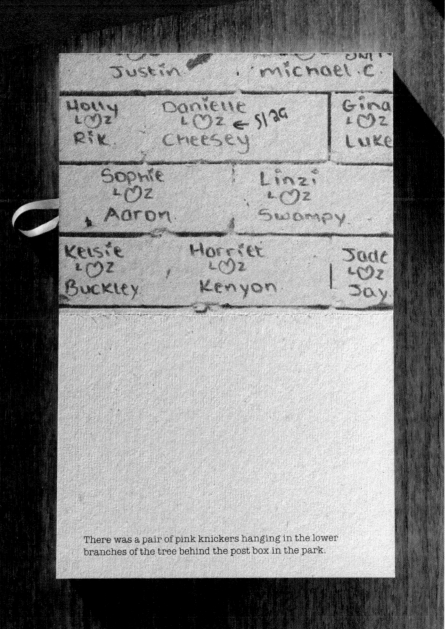

There was a pair of pink knickers hanging in the lower branches of the tree behind the post box in the park.

Left: Front and back cover of Where Are You? A Postman's Diary.

Above, center: A spread featuring the photography of Shaw + Shaw as well as the writing of Kevin Boniface.

Above, right: Found information printed on rough card.

"We wanted to create an almost throwaway feel to the book, as if each leaf was scribbled on the back of a cigarette packet or a piece of card found lying around."

Dave Simpson, Love

'Mad-Dog' was hanging around the landing wanting a lift home in a Leece Rd van. After a while he began to get impatient.

"...Fuckin Hell! C'mon someone give us a lift or I'm gonna have to walk home through all the slags and prozzies."

Then he mimed a really purposeful, steadfast walk-on-the-spot whilst shouting, "No love, I don't want a fucking blow-job, out me way!...Thank you."

In the canteen I had some toast and coffee (£1.13).

"Ooh, I could've saved you some money there" said the woman serving on. "We used to have an offer on, it were really good value. You got two bits of toast and jam, cereal or porridge, fruit juice and tea or coffee for a pound. It were called, erm, what were it? - erm - 'The Healthy Option'. It were a good offer that but we don't do it any more - it's a shame that, it's a lot of money that really."

Dave Higson was stood eating chips and curry sauce at the gates to the yard. I asked him what he was up to.
"Well I was sat over there under that pink tree," he said pointing to a cherry tree in blossom, "but I kept getting fucking pink bits in me tea so I've come over here."

Kevin Boniface works as a postman (mailman) in the town of Huddersfield in the north of England. He is also an artist, writer, and illustrator, drawing on his experiences working for the Royal Mail to collate scraps of information, found or written, that comment on everyday life in the area.

The resulting work manages to be both a hilarious commentary on and joyous example of the sarcastic and crude wit of northern England. For an exhibition at the Lichtaffen Gallery in London, he collaborated with old friends, the photographers Jo and Christoph Shaw, to produce a dense exhibition as well as a book that would both document the exhibition and have an afterlife as an object in its own right.

The book was designed by Dave Simpson, then creative director of Love, a design and advertising agency based in Manchester. To preserve the random and eclectic nature of the materials involved in the show, as well as maintaining its sense of wit, he decided to use a diverse series of stocks, from the cheapest and roughest to the most glossy and luxurious, loosely binding them together in a form reminiscent of a block of tear-off notes.

"We wanted to create an almost throwaway feel to the book, as if each leaf was scribbled on the back of a cigarette packet or a piece of card found lying around," says Simpson. "Hence the use of papers and boards more often found as packing materials, carton boards, newsprint, and so on. The finished item was bounded in the least obtrusive way, so that each postcard maintained its own individual characteristic."

The book has sold well in specialist graphics bookstores, and won several design awards.

Copywriting and illustration: Kevin Boniface
Photos: Shaw + Shaw Photography
Images: Courtesy of Love

Far left: Another spread combining photography and writing to amusing effect, this time on smoother paper stock.

Left: Further spread from the book.

Top, center: Two found notes reprinted in the book.

Top, right: Another spread where the design adds to the comic effect.

Project
Paperworld 2007
Design
Kram/Weisshaar
Client
**Messe Frankfurt
Exhibition GmbH**

**Left: View of the champagne bar
at Paperworld, with graffiti artist
Mode 2 at work in the background.**

Internationale Frankfurter Messe, Frankfurt

"We wanted to structure the space to break the military order of regular blocks and inject some of the architectural excitement of a city into the exhibition."

Clemens Weisshaar, Kram/Weisshaar

Left: Aerial view showing the distinctive carpet graphics.

Trade fairs can all too easily become dull affairs, so when cutting edge digital design partnership Kram/Weisshaar took on the brief to design the 2007 Paperworld fair (catering to the office and stationery supply industry) in Frankfurt, Germany, they decided to draw on their interactive skills to create a more lively and involving experience. Or, in the words of Clemens Weisshaar and Reed Kram, their master plan was about "reinjecting momentum into the mechanics of the trade fair."

"It is a giant hall; it's very, very large and the exhibition was all about pens and pencils, so there was this polarity of scale," explains Clemens Weisshaar. "We wanted to structure the space to break the military order of regular blocks and inject some of the architectural excitement of a city into the exhibition." At the same time as visitors walked around the cavernous, 55,000 square yard (50,000 square meter) exhibition halls—guided by wayfinding graphics integrated into the carpet—a variety of interrelated features playfully engaged them while staying close to the matter in hand.

Mode 2, a well-known graffiti and street artist, could be seen—suspended from a motorized cradle—painting a 175 square yard (160 square meter) mural around the champagne bar. Filmed and projected onto a cinema-sized screen, everyone could follow the completion of the mural as it unfolded over the five days of the fair. For a similar thematic resonance, Luigi Colani, the eccentric German designer who has been creating sveltely organic and streamlined products since the 1950s, was commissioned to create a giant pen structure, some 23 feet (7 meters) high. A total of 58 oversized pens formed a "hall of fame" along the central corridor of the fair.

Lead designers: Clemens Weisshaar and Reed Kram with Dennis Bangert and Khashayar Naimanan
Guest designers: Mode 2 (mural), Luigi Colani (pen sculpture)
Graphics: Kram/Weisshaar
Photos: Frank Stolle, courtesy of Kram/Weisshaar

Top, left: Close-up showing Mode 2's "Work in Progress" in action.

Top, center: The giant pen sculpture designed by Luigi Colani.

Top, right: View showing the large screen to the left.

Bottom, right: Computer simulation showing the relationship between the screen and Mode 2 at work.

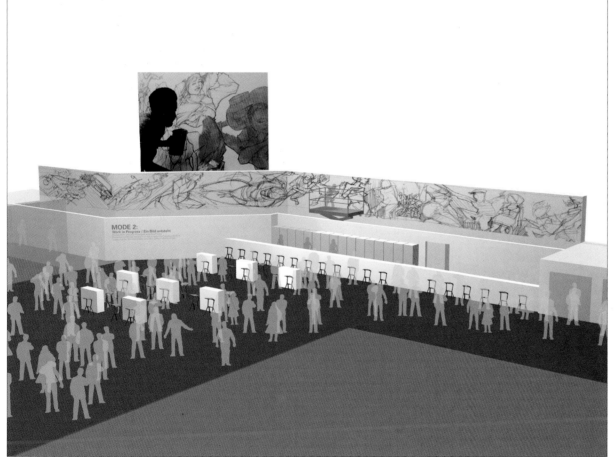

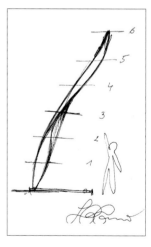

Above: Luigi Colani's sketch for the sculpture.

"Visitors walked around
the exhibition halls—guided
by wayfinding graphics
integrated into the carpet
—a variety of interrelated
features playfully engaged
them while staying close
to the matter in hand."

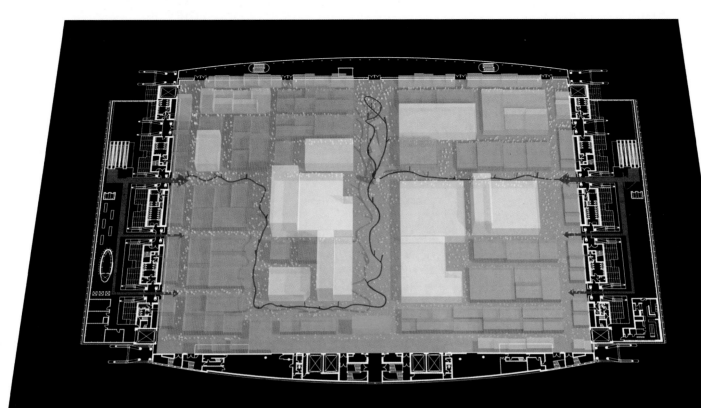

Left-hand page, and image left:
Details of the carpet graphics
and wayfinding.

Above: Kram/Weisshaar's
masterplan for the trade show.

"The trailer arrives in small towns, educating about mining through oral histories, and actively seeks new miners to interview."

Jake Barton, Local Projects

Project
The Miners' Story Project

Design
Local Projects

Client
Flandrau Science Center

MINERS ‹STORY› PROJECT

The Miners' Story Project will preserve and share stories about life in mines and mining communities in the Southwest U.S.

Above: The copper-clad trailer of the Miners' Story Project traveled around Arizona and New Mexico.

Above: A welcoming door into
a space that also functions as
a recording studio documenting the
personal accounts of the miners.

Few exhibitions can more fully claim the title of traveling show than this, the Miners' Story Project. Essentially a trailer that travels around mining communities in Arizona and New Mexico, its tasks are to act as a recording space to gather and preserve stories (and artifacts) from miners and the mines they worked in, and also to share these with visitors, largely school parties.

The eye-catching caravan, entirely clad in copper, also acts to publicize the project, which culminates in the new Mineral Museum at the Flandrau Science Center. "The trailer's main feature is a profile portrait of a copper miner, made up of water-jet cut holes that are actually perforations for a giant speaker, which plays oral histories at each stop," explains Jake Barton, principal of New York–based Local Projects. "The trailer arrives in small towns, promoting the project, educating about mining through oral histories, and actively seeks new miners to interview."

It is a design that is as much interactive as it is a traditional exhibition space, a development of the approach Local Projects created for its well-received StoryCorps booth installed at New York's Grand Central Terminal for the Library of Congress.

Bottom, right: The trailer on one of its many stops.

Top, right: The trailer on a different location, showing the pixellated holes of the images of the miner that doubled as speaker holes.

"This project aims to turn the museum inside out, into a feedback loop that engages the public into making content, in a hyper-local way that activates small, rural communities in a novel and engaging way. It educates and collects stories, one small town at a time, and apparently gets the most amazing comments at gas stations."

Jake Barton, Local Projects

"While museum artifacts can be spectacular on their own, these gems and minerals are made universally amazing through the human narratives associated with them," says Barton. "This project aims to turn the museum inside out, into a feedback loop that engages the public into making content, in a hyper-local way that activates small, rural communities in a novel and engaging way.

"It educates and collects stories, one small town at a time, and apparently gets the most amazing comments at gas stations."

Images: Courtesy of Local Projects

Right: School children listening to the accounts of miners being broadcast through the holes of the pixellated image of a miner on the trailer's exterior.

Project
Signage for the City Museum at Old Treasury

Design
emerystudio

"The sign forms were designed to minimize any penetration into the historic steps. Some conservative members of the public did not appreciate the approach."

Garry Emery, emerystudio

The City Museum at Old Treasury in Melbourne is housed in an imposing building that is considered one of the finest examples of nineteenth-century architecture in Australia. And while it has a prominent location in the city, there was a problem: the main entry to the museum is through an insignificant door that is found only after climbing a grand flight of steps and crossing a windswept podium.

So emerystudio was briefed to find a way of signaling the presence of the museum, encouraging visitors, and announcing temporary exhibitions and operating building fabric. "The brightly colored, folded monumental signage elements are designed as contemporary insertions into the historic setting," explains Garry Emery.

Left: Side view of the signage, showing how it is installed on the steps.

Client
The City Museum at Old Treasury

Location
Melbourne

"These sign objects are located to subtly guide people upward to discover the museum entry and the exhibitions as well as branding the museum."

While bold and dynamic, the signage remains sensitive to the conservation requirements, something that was not universally appreciated. "The sign forms were designed to minimize any penetration into the historic steps. Some more conservative members of the public did not appreciate the approach," Emery notes wryly.

The trapezoidal shape of the signage was also developed to provide a corporate identity for the City Museum to use in its print and web communications. The signage itself was constructed from 25mm and 40mm plate steel, with the text masked and sprayed on.

Designers: Garry Emery, Mark Janetzki
Fabrication: Robert Hook
Photos: Paul Knight

Left: One of the signage elements that alert visitors to the City Museum behind.

"We used a bountiful array of color which introduces the attraction at the entrance and separates the thematic zones. Through the use of eccentric circles, the graphic language was developed to illustrate the sonic boom."

Julie Vander Herberg, Reich + Petch

Project
Barbados Concorde Experience

Design
Reich + Petch

Client
Barbados Tourism Investment Inc.

Barbados Concorde Experience

Location
Grantley Adams International Airport, Barbados

Left: Alpha Echo, a decommissioned Concorde is, quite literally, the centerpiece of the show.

Above: Visitors watching film of Concorde in action projected on to the fuselage of the aircraft.

There are few objects that have captured the public imagination as much as Concorde. Barbados, as one of the supersonic aircraft's regular ports of call before its untimely withdrawal from service, is therefore a fitting location for a visitor experience dedicated to it. In a converted hangar adjacent to the Grantley Adams International Airport, where Concorde would arrive every Saturday, the display is based around Alpha Echo, a decommissioned aircraft in British Airways livery.

The visitor experience takes in the history of passenger flight as well as the history of its star exhibit. To recreate the noise and excitement of Concorde in action, film footage is projected on to the fuselage of Alpha Echo. Visitors can also enter inside the aircraft, sit in the seats and watch a presentation, or pretend to fly the aircraft themselves at a flight simulator. Colorful lighting and graphics were used to enliven the space, which could always threaten to be just a hangar with an airplane parked inside it. Decorating the outside of the hangar with an image of Concorde also injected an element of drama into proceedings.

"We used a bountiful array of color which introduces the attraction at the entrance and separates the thematic zones. Through the use of eccentric circles, the graphic language was developed to illustrate the

Left: A history of air flight was presented with minimal exhibits.

sonic boom. Large-format information and thematic banners, graphic info rails, and multimedia displays visually interpret the exhibit story," explains Julie Vander Herberg, who worked on the graphics alongside project director Whit Petch at Toronto-based consultancy Reich + Petch.

Other designers: Science North and Core Designs
Images: Courtesy of Reich + Petch

Top, left: Entrance to the Barbados Concorde Experience.

Top, center: The experience is heavily dependent on graphic sleight of hand.

Top, right: Invites to the opening of the Barbados Concorde Experience were in the form of airline tickets.

Above: Overview of the central display of the Barbados Concorde Experience.

Project
Sonance Trade Show Exhibit

Design
Pentagram

Client
Sonance

Location
CEDIA Expo, Denver

"Unusually, the collaborations on the project were nearly all in-house, as Pentagram colleagues were not only responsible for Sonance's new corporate identity, but also for its website and the product design."
Lorenzo Apicella, Pentagram

Far left: Overview of the Sonance stand at the CEDIA Expo, showing the interplay between the new logo and the exhibit architecture.

Left: End view of the exhibit, showing the way in which perspective was used to match the new logotype.

When Sonance, which sells upmarket integrated speaker systems, took a stand at the CEDIA Expo for custom electronics in 2006, not only did it want an impressive exhibit, but it also wanted to present a new logo and corporate identity to the world.

So Lorenzo Apicella and his team at Pentagram's San Francisco offices came up with the idea of using the squares of the new logo as the basis of the exhibit. "The form of this design sought to embody the spirit of Sonance's new identity three-dimensionally," says Apicella. "It also had to anticipate the functional needs of a number of future smaller exhibit locations, and therefore had to be scalable."

The high-level open square volumes were lit internally, and bespoke fabrics were stretched over aluminum frames which were deliberately left exposed to give a structural sense. They were also lit internally, and placed off-axis for perspectival effects and impact from wherever the stand was viewed. This also allowed the placement of hospitality booths alongside the main display, together with a large curved information desk. The overall floor space measured 80 by 40 feet (24.3 by 12.1 meters).

Left: Detail of rooms below the cubes with classic furniture and bamboo floors, showing the in-wall speaker systems that were being launched.

Top, center: A curved information desk greeted visitors as they entered the exhibit area.

The installations below the cubes take their footprint from the overhead structure, and were kitted out with classic furniture and bamboo floors to reinforce the design-conscious brand values.

Unusually, says Apicella, the collaborations on the project were nearly all in-house, as Pentagram colleagues were not only responsible for Sonance's new corporate identity, but also for its website and the product design.

Lead designers: Lorenzo Apicella, Matthew Clare, Jason McCombs
Fabricator: Sparks Exhibits
Budget: $500,000 US
Photos: Jamie Padgett

Top, right: Different furniture was specified for each of the "rooms" under the color-filled cubes.

Right: Detail showing the information booths in the background.

Project
Musée d'Art Moderne Grand-Duc Jean (Mudam)

Architecture
I.M. Pei of Pei Cobb Freed & Partners

Above: Inside view of I. M. Pei's light-filled structure. Both images courtesy of Musée d'Art Moderne Grand-Duc Jean. Architect: I.M. Pei. Photography © André Weisgerber.

Right: Exterior of Mudam, designed by I. M. Pei. The site was originally an eighteenth-century fort.

Musée d'Art Moderne Grand-Duc Jean (Mudam)

Client
Grand Duchy of Luxembourg

Location
Luxembourg

An all-star cast was gathered to create a museum that would not only honor the 25-year reign of the now abdicated Grand-Duc Jean, but also create a vibrant institution that would give the small Duchy of Luxembourg some cultural prestige to match its importance as a financial center.

Apart from the static and impressive arrow-shaped architecture, designed by I.M. Pei, the aim was to create a genuinely creative and fluid organization. The ambitious idea behind this €90 million project was to blur the conventional division between the standard "support" furniture of a museum and privileged displayed object in the creation of an art space. So various artists and designers were brought in to collaborate on different aspects of the museum and their contributions exist as part of the content in their own right.

Take, for instance, the website (www.mudam.lu), created by French digital artist and designer Claude Closky, which prioritizes quirkiness and aesthetics over the usual functional museum approach. While announcing the museum's avant garde aspirations with its blankness, the website also includes a simple yet ingenious and easily navigable online gallery space, which cleverly maintains the three-dimensional feel of a traditional exhibition space. It also hosts a vibrant magazine "edited" by Closky.

Top, left: The museum's logo, designed by Ott + Stein, with a bespoke font by Oliver Peters.

Top, right: The central seating area of the Mudam Café design by the Bouroullec brothers, incorporating a roof made of felt tiles by Kvadrat. Photo © Erwan and Ronan Bouroullec.

Musée d'Art Moderne Grand-Duc Jean (Mudam)

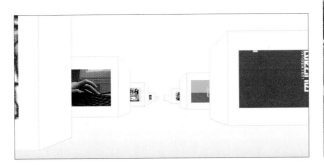

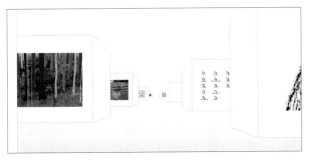

MUDAM IN ENGLISH. MUDAM EN FRANÇAIS. SEARCH . The programme, practical information, about this site, the museum, the collection, the publications, Mudam Café & Boutique, Mudam education, the press, support Mudam, the team, join us, F.A.Q, the downloads, communications, the newsletter, the links, The iGallery, the magazine.

The store and restaurant, designed by celebrity designer brothers Erwan and Ronan Bouroullec, has a deliberately provisional quality, as if it could be reinstalled at any point. Drawing on an earlier display for textile manufacturer Kvadrat, the brothers used felt tiles on a wooden structure to achieve the desired effect.

Mudam's logo, designed by Berlin-based graphic design consultancy Ott + Stein, also signals the uncompromising aspirations of the museum, using a bespoke font designed separately by Oliver Peters which emulates Japanese script, giving Mudam's communications a distinctive flavor.

Café and store design: Ronan & Erwan Bouroullec Design
Web design: Claude Closky
Logo design: Ott + Stein
Font design: Oliver Peters
Lighting: Ove Arup & Partners

Bottom, left: The Mudam Café designed by Erwan and Ronan Bouroullec. Photo © Erwan and Ronan Bouroullec.

Left, top and center: Two sequences from the "iGallery" on Mudam's website, designed by Claude Closky.

Left, bottom: The homepage of Mudam's playful website designed by Claude Closky, at www.mudam.lu

Top, right: Another view of the exterior of Mudam. Image courtesy of Musée d'Art Moderne Grand-Duc Jean. Architect: I.M. Pei. Photography © André Weisgerber.

Above: Another image of the central seating area of the Mudam Café design by the Bouroullec brothers, incorporating a roof made of felt tiles by Kvadrat. Photo © Erwan and Ronan Bouroullec.

Right: Detail of the interior staircase. Image courtesy of Musée d'Art Moderne Grand-Duc Jean. Architect: I.M. Pei. Photography © André Weisgerber.

Musée d'Art Moderne Grand-Duc Jean (Mudam)

"The impressive arrow-shaped building designed by I.M. Pei occupies a site that was once an eighteenth-century fort."

"I wanted to create a project that was a demonstration of sustainability, and this is what came out of that desire."
Mark Randall

Project
Urban Forest

Design
185 different designers contributed

Client
AIGA/NY
Location
New York

Left: John Pirman's banner for the Urban Forest project in situ in Times Square, joining in the noise.

Above, left: The banner designed by Rob Alexander.

Above, right: Handbag by Jack Spade, recyled from Rob Alexander's banner (left).

The idea was a simple but powerful one. Get designers and artists to create banners that would be hung in and around Times Square in New York, using visual means to make a powerful statement about sustainability. Not only did the banners make their political point in a bewildering variety of ways, demonstrating the richness of graphic design let loose, but they also interacted in many unexpected ways with the existing architectural fauna of the metropolis, showing how this urban environment too could be transformed into an impromptu exhibition space.

"We invited specific designers that we wanted to participate, and then we had an open call to members of the AIGA. We did not want it to be invitation only or a competition," says Mark Randall, one of the project team and a key instigator of Urban Forest. "The response was totally unexpected—basically everyone we invited said yes. Within two weeks we had over 300 designers say they wanted to do it, so we stopped asking since we only had the potential for 200 participants. In the end, 185 came through which was perfect."

From the inception of the project the intention was to make products out of the banners to sell once the exhibition was over. "I wanted to create some kind of a project that was a demonstration of sustainability, and

Left: A pigeon joining in with the banner created by Goodesign.

Top, left: Banner designed by Go Welsh.
Top, center: Perspectival play on the banner designed by John Gall.
Top, right: Banner designed by Graphic Design for Love.

this is what came out of that desire," says Randall. One of the contributors, Alan Dye, was also creative director of bag design company Jack Spade, so it was natural for that company to produce the handbags. The banners were recycled in such a way that each transformed into two tote bags. T-shirts featuring the various designs were also available, and profits from the merchandise sales went to AIGA/NY's student mentoring project.

The success of the project has seen it emulated in cities across the US.

Photos: Mark Dye Photography

Top: More of the bags made from recycled banners.
Top, right: The banner designed by KesselsKramer.

Right: The banners were layed out alphabetically, as shown on this map.

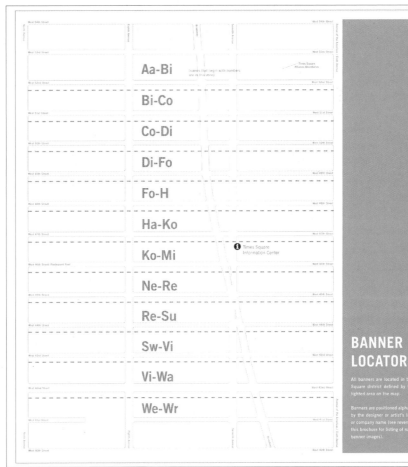

Right: Lyndon and Rick Valicenti's banner in situ.

**Center: Banner by Rodrigo Corral making its point elegantly in context.
Far right: Banner created by Omar Vulpinari.**

Urban Forest

DESIGN TIMES SQUARE:
THE URBAN FOREST PROJECT

RODRIGO CORRAL

DESIGN TIMES SQUARE:
THE URBAN FOREST PROJECT

OMAR VULPINARI

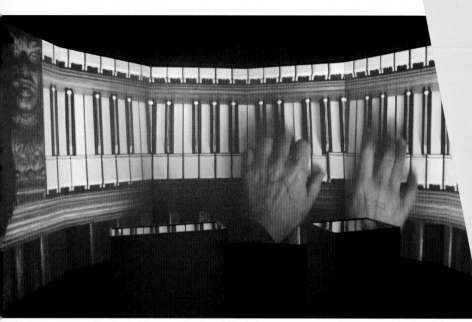

Project
Bachhaus

Design
atelierbrückner

Bachhaus

Client
Neue Bachgesellschaft

Location
Eisenach

"Our design approach was to ensure that Bach's music always frames the visitor experience. You always hear what you see. The visitor is not a consumer but a participator."

Uwe Brückner, atelierbrückner

To mark a century since its foundation, the Bachhaus in Eisenach built a new wing (designed by Penkhues Architekten) which almost doubled the exhibition space. The new exhibition design therefore had to connect the two wings, while also demonstrating the musicological and performance heritage of J. S. Bach's music, and the abstract, almost mathematical, nature of many of his compositions. "And it had to work equally well for the connoisseur as well as for people with little knowledge of classical music or of Bach," adds Professor Uwe Brückner.

Brückner was keen to avoid using words to explain musical scores and materials. "Our design approach was to ensure that Bach's music always frames the visitor experience. You always hear what you see," he says.

But the danger was that there would be a cacophony. To solve this potential problem, music is projected from small speakers with narrowly defined range, near the relevant exhibits. Alternatively, visitors can choose to sit in strategically placed Bubble chairs and select the tracks of music they would like to listen to on headphones.

And to avoid a visual cacophony, Brückner and his team chose to limit themselves to using aluminum and acrylic to emulate the intellectual purity of Bach's music.

Top, left: The interior of the central display, the Accessible Piece of Music—created together with Marc Tamschick—showing the oversize projection of an organist playing. The delicate manuscripts and scores in the exhibition cases in front are protected from light during the projection. Photograph by André Nestler.

Bottom, left: Eero Aarnio's iconic Bubble chairs are fitted with audio equipment to allow visitors to listen to a selection of Bach's music. Photograph by Uwe Ditz.

Above, center: The exterior of the Accessible Piece of Music, with a display of facsimiles around its perimeter. Photograph by Uwe Ditz.

The centerpiece of the permanent exhibition is an installation called the "Accessible Piece of Music," designed to allow an intimate experience with Bach's music. Inside this display, the visitor sees a large screen showing organ music being played, but shot from unusual angles, such as above the hands. "It creates an immersive feeling, one of participation in the performance. The visitor is not a consumer but a participator," explains Brückner.

This installation also houses some rare and delicate autograph scores, but these are protected by lids while the "performance" takes place and by very low lighting levels at other times.

The luminescent white exterior of the structure has a display of backlit facsimiles, whose open status clearly demarcates them from the originals. Brückner is particularly proud of the way the museum allows the nonexpert to interact with the music of Bach in this design that he calls "sophisticated, quiet, focused, and experiential."

Top, left: The display of portraits of Bach, showing the display cases and captioning system. Photograph by Uwe Ditz.

Bottom, left: A luminescent display of historical instruments in a room in the original building. Photograph by Uwe Ditz.

Bachhaus

Top: A large-scale city panorama of Eisenach as Bach would have known it forms the main display in one of the rooms of the original building. Photograph by Uwe Ditz.

Above, left: Detail showing the simple and pure approach to presenting artifacts relating to Bach's life. Photograph by Uwe Ditz.

Above, right: Detail of one of the display cases, featuring coins with magnification. Photograph by Uwe Ditz.

"Fiberglass rods, giving the appearance of tendons, were tethered together and spanned the exhibition space, transforming it and seemingly creating connections between different parts of the show."

"Explicit and encoded processes within design" was the dauntingly theoretical subtitle for ScriptedbyPurpose, an exhibition staged to collect together a new generation of designers and architects whose work is reliant on computer script. Marc Fornes, the architect behind the show, approached the challenge of presenting work as abstract as this with the creation of a single overarching gesture that would give cohesion to the grand, and very traditional, architecture of the F.U.E.L. Collection in Philadelphia's Old City.

Fiberglass rods, giving the appearance of tendons, were tethered together and spanned the exhibition space, transforming it and creating the impression of connections between different parts of the show.

Left and right: Visitors in the main atrium of the F.U.E.L. exhibition space, which was crisscrossed by fiberglass tendons.

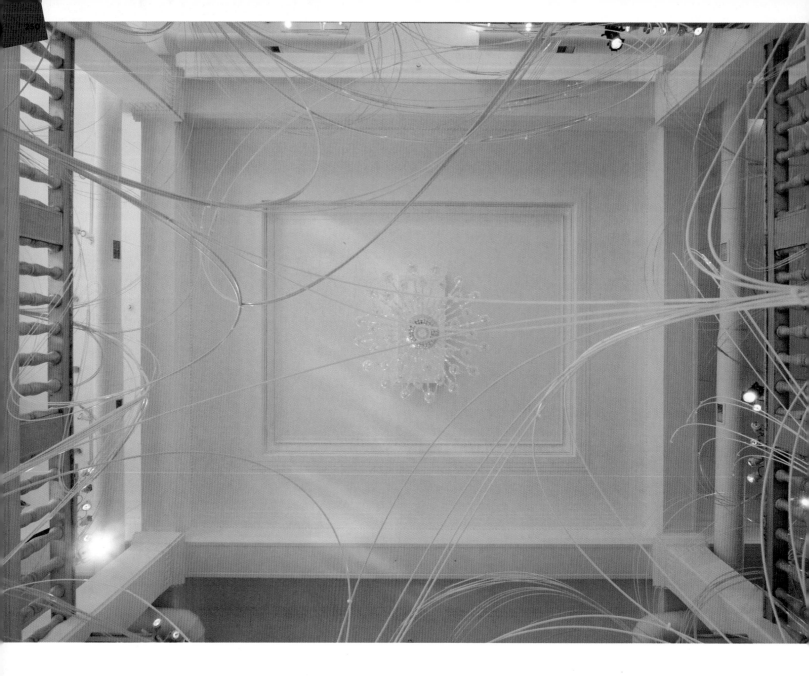

**Above: The view up from the
cushions in the center of the space.**

**Top, center: Hanging display boards
and floor-based labeling.**

It was an ingenious, and low-tech, solution. It is also reminiscent of the 2005 installation designed by Zaha Hadid (in whose studio Fornes had formerly worked) for Design.05 Miami, in which large white organic sinews traversed the internal atrium of the converted Moore Building like giant pieces of chewing gum.

Apart from requiring that all the submitted projects should involve scripting techniques, Fornes also wanted to ensure that it wasn't merely a talk shop on technique, and asked that all the exhibitors presented the codes and tools they had used as open source alongside their work. "Set up like some sort of 'cellular automata' system, the submissions process for that exhibition was based on those two rules of thumb only in order to collect an 'emergent' spectrum of work within the field of scripting and design process," says Fornes.

Production team: Jonathan Proto, Brandon Kruysman, Andrew Warner, Jared Laucks
Photos: Nate Kalushner

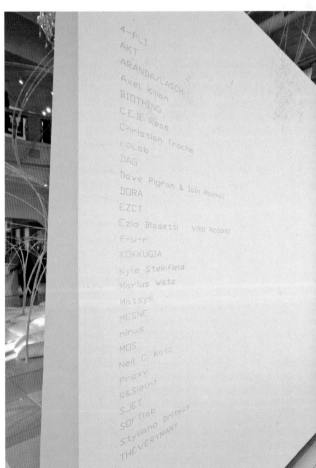

Top, right: The "tendons" traveled through much of the available exhibition space.

Bottom, right: Simple exhibition furniture was used for much of the show, such as this with the names of the 20 featured designers.

"We wanted to create a sense of awe. You could lie down and look at the ceiling and see the painting from the same distance as Michelangelo would have when he was painting the Sistine Chapel."

Stephen Greenberg, Metaphor

Project
Michelangelo Drawings: Closer to the Master

Design
Metaphor

49

Michelangelo Drawings: Closer to the Master

Left: Projection was used to show visitors the Sistine Chapel ceiling in the appropriate aspect and, by lying down on the bench, they could view the work from exactly the same distance as Michelangelo would have seen it himself.

Above: The design emulates a Renaissance library and avoids the usual dim lighting of drawings exhibitions. Original sixteenth-century colors were sourced from the Vatican, such as the green background painted in original paints by the artist Antony Malinowski to Michelangelo's only surviving full-size cartoon.

Michelangelo's drawings are some of the most prized and famous in existence. So putting together a show for the British Museum that could convey their context and function while preserving some sense of intimacy with the visitor, and also manage not to be gimmicky or tacky, was a formidable challenge.

"We wanted to create a sense of awe," explains Stephen Greenberg, a director at Metaphor. "You could lie down and look at the ceiling and see the painting from the same distance as Michelangelo would have when he was painting the Sistine Chapel." This was made possible by the use of projection, which also created a sense of intimacy with the recreated Sistine Chapel ceiling for the visitor. Details from the Sistine Chapel ceiling and sketches for it were projected on to a false ceiling some 8 feet (2.5 meters) high.

The overall concept was to create a serious yet light space reminiscent of a Renaissance library, with simple lecterns grouped in alcoves to afford some level of intimacy with the rarely displayed drawings. With the assistance of the Vatican, original fresco colors and paints were used to heighten the emotional impact of key works while giving further historical resonance.

Top and bottom, right: Vistas were created so people could look from the drawings to the final artifact, as here with photographs of the dome of St. Peters and the Medici Tomb.

The displays were deliberately old-fashioned in their labeling.

Michelangelo Drawings: Closer to the Master

"We wanted to avoid the usual dark environment for a drawings show," says Greenberg. "We used off-white MDF for the exhibition furniture, allowing the drawings to stand out themselves. By lighting the floor, the show felt very light despite the very low (less than 50 lux) lighting levels required for the conservation of these priceless treasures. People couldn't believe that they were at a drawings exhibition."

He adds that focal lengths were carefully considered so as to ease the visitor experience, particularly for the slightly older demographic anticipated for the show. The labels and the drawing are at the same length, and vistas were created to allow people to see the drawing or sketch and a large-scale photograph of the final artifact or building behind it.

Photos: Hufton + Crow

Top: Michelangelo's final three studies of the Crucifixion were presented on a wall painted in graphite by Malinowksi to create a Rothko-esque atmosphere.

Right: A graphics-heavy timeline circumnavigated the exhibition along the perimeter walls.

Above: One of the graphics explaining the Sistine Chapel ceiling. The stands were made of off-white MDF, and housed lighting that was bounced off the floor.

Right: Another view of the central projection installation.

Far right: Overview showing the relation of the different aspects of the exhibition design.

"By lighting the floor, the show felt very light despite the very low (less than 50 lux) lighting levels required for the conservation of these priceless treasures. People couldn't believe that they were at a drawings exhibition."

Stephen Greenberg, Metaphor

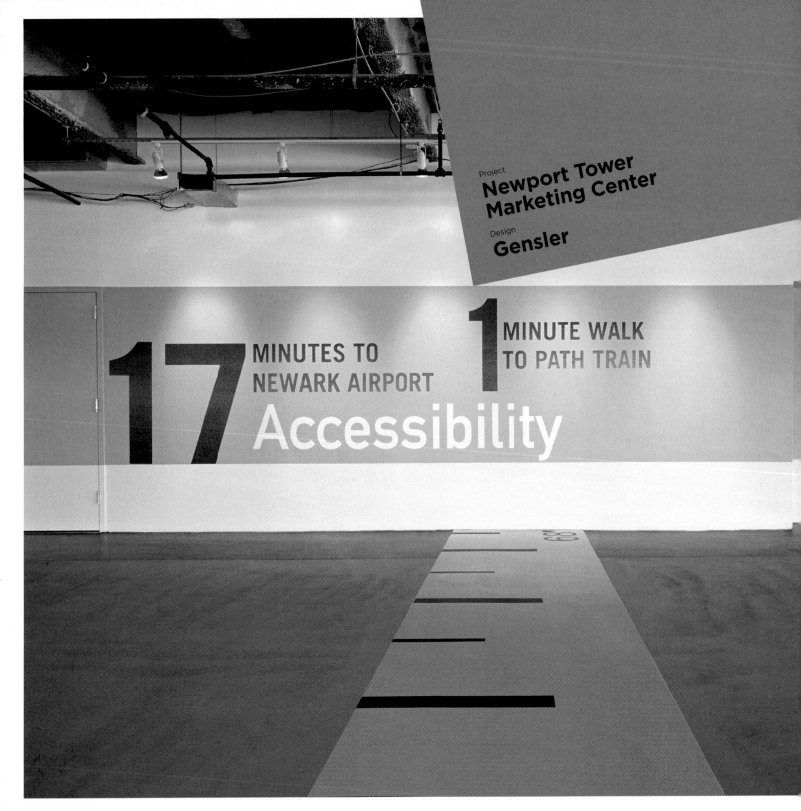

Project
**Newport Tower
Marketing Center**

Design
Gensler

17 MINUTES TO
NEWARK AIRPORT

1 MINUTE WALK
TO PATH TRAIN

Accessibility

Client
TrizecHahn Newport

Location
Jersey City

Left: Overview of the empty floor space that is vividly transformed by oversized graphics giving relevant information to prospective tenants and brokers.

Above: Gestures were limited to where they would have most impact, and used bold colors to maximum advantage.

Flexibility

CAN ACCOMMODATE

TENANTS FROM

5,000 TO 300,000 SQ. FT.

36%

THE COST OF
MIDTOWN MANHATTAN

Many marketing centers aspire to the condition of an exhibition, but precious few achieve it. Presenting empty office space to prospective clients can be a pedestrian business, but when TrizecHahn, then owners of the 36-story Newport Tower in New Jersey, approached Gensler, it was decided that, despite a limited budget, a much more daring approach would be taken.

Gensler, drawing on its expertise in office design, drew up a test-fit plan for the entire available space, and then decided which areas to showcase, leaving indications of how the remaining areas could be used. By using some techniques more common to exhibition design, Gensler was able to make it easier for visitors to imagine how the space would look once it was fitted out.

"It was designed as an exhibition-type space where we minimally transformed raw space and juxtaposed the unfinished loft-like space with finished zones and vibrant graphics," says Thomas Vecchione. "Our installations were successful in helping tenants visualize what they could achieve within the space and highlighted the building's attributes and features with a fresh perspective. By highlighting key areas within the marketing center, we engaged the visitor with elements of surprise and impactful information along 'the tour.'"

Left: Simple floor paint and applied graphics transformed the empty office space.

Top: Only a few areas were fitted out so that clients could get a feel for the finished space.

> "Creating large gestures in focused areas on a large floorplate allowed us to cover more ground with a limited budget."

Thomas Vecchione, Gensler

And creating large gestures in focused areas on a large floorplate allowed us to cover more ground with a limited budget."

The exhibition was closely coordinated with a wider communication strategy, which included invitations, brochures, media presentations, and corporate hospitality. Gensler says its unusual approach to real estate presentation allowed the Newport Tower to stand out from its competitors as well as motivating the brokers involved in looking for tenants for the space.

Designers: Thomas Vecchione, Shih Hua Liong
Images: Courtesy of Gensler

Top, right: Overview of the space, showing effective use of a giant tape measure graphic.

Right: Much of the space remained empty.

Project
London College of Fashion Graduate Show

Design
Moving Brands

"We wanted to do something unusual for the LCF, so our proposal for the stand was centered around a 26 ¼ foot long, interactive table showcasing the work of nearly 200 students. Each student was assigned a cube holding their personal details and up to five pieces of work each."

Guy Wolstenholme, **Moving Brands**

Top, left: Visitors engaging with the interactive table at the 2006 London College of Fashion degree show.
Bottom, left: The design had to work in a busy environment full of visitors.

Right: The interactive table, showing the color groupings.

London College of Fashion Graduate Show

Client
London College of Fashion

Location
London

Graduate shows are important launch pads for students in creative fields, so creating the correct platform to display their work is critical. When Moving Brands, a combined design and media agency, was approached to design the graduate show for the London College of Fashion, the brief was succinct: "showcase all the students work in a clear, comprehensive, and impactful way."

Moving Brands was mindful of the competing graduate shows and decided to do something that would make this show stand out from the rest. "We wanted to do something unusual for the LCF, so our proposal for the stand was centered around an 8 meter [26 ¼ foot] long, interactive table showcasing the work of nearly 200 students," says Guy Wolstenholme, design director on the project. "Each student was assigned a cube holding their personal details and up to five pieces of work each."

By moving their hand across the virtual cube, it would change to show different work. The students were grouped in colors according to the different courses they had completed, so visitors could select what they wanted to see by category as well as by individual. As well as being an intuitive and attention-grabbing device, the interactive table was able to present much

Top, left and bottom, left: Details of the interactive table.

Top, center and top, right: Details showing the backstage wiring the installation required.

"The design of the show was well received and lightly modified, primarily by use of different color, for the next year's graduate show."

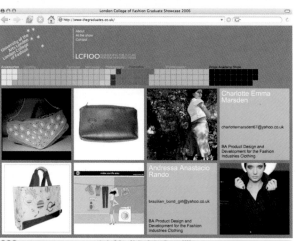

more detailed information about any particular one of the nearly 200 students to the interested visitor than would otherwise have been the case.

This virtual, database-derived, display architecture meant that the show was readily translatable online for an accompanying website. The design of the show was well received and lightly modified, primarily by use of different color, for the next year's graduate show.

Lead designers: James Bull, Guy Wolstenholme, Karsten Schmidt, Davin Gormley
Images: Courtesy of Moving Brands

Left: The accompanying website was able to closely match the physical presence of the graduate show.

"My goal for the show was to create an environment that encouraged people to stay in the space, not just to view the work, but also to view each other and interact."

Bryan Metzdorf

Project
All That is Solid Melts into Air

Design
Bryan Metzdorf

Above: Eschewing the customary production values, this low-budget collaboration used the format of an exhibition to create something that functioned almost as a work of installation art in itself.

Right: A disparate series of low-tech interactives were an integral part of the show.

All that is solid melts into air, all that is holy is profaned, and man is at last compelled to face with sober senses his real condition of life and his relations with his kind

Karl Marx

All That is Solid Melts into Air

Completed in a mere seven days, this show was the result of a close collaboration between a curator and an artist who both studied at the School of the Art Institute of Chicago.

Bryan Metzdorf, who studied designed objects, had already worked once with curator Emma Balazs, but the guiding theme for this show was to be "the ephemeral nature of being." A total of 30 friends, primarily artists, made the project happen in such a short time frame and to a very small budget.

To convey the idea of fragility and historical dissolution implied by the famous quote of Karl Marx that was used as the show's title, Metzdorf chose to deck the space out in various layers of patterns, reflections, and stencils, all abstracted from relevant materials that he and Balazs had collated for the exhibition.

"My goal for the show was to create an environment that encouraged people to stay in the space, not just to view the work, but also to view each other and interact," Metzdorf explains. "Art is always seen in a context, even the sort of vacuum that is the traditional gallery is a context. Given this idea, my aim was to create a setting which united the works with the space and the curator's theme."

The show, both in subject matter and form, evolved out of close collaboration. "Coming from a background in film directing, where I worked closely with a production designer, this seemed natural. It was only after our first show together, which attracted so much interest from artists and other visitors, that I realized this wasn't standard exhibition practice," says Balazs. "The visitors' responses to this project encouraged us to pursue this approach to exhibition making, which as someone commented, is as much an art practice itself as it is the work of a curator and designer."

Photos: Courtesy of James Prinz and the School of the Art Institute of Chicago, Gallery 2, and Project Space

---

Top, left: The stencils and paintings were executed by friends of the designer.

Bottom, left: The Karl Marx quote that inspired the show's title was also painted over a doorway.

Top, center: Framed artwork was very clearly "curated."

Top, right: A corner bookshelf was one of the exhibits.

A big thank you to the many designers who took time to share information about their projects and supply images of their work. Collaborating with the team at RotoVision and Form was a real pleasure, and I would like to particularly thank my commissioning editor Liz Farrelly and project editor Jane Roe for their friendly support while working on this book.

John Stones